VICTORIAN & EDWARDIAN
LOCOMOTIVES

VICTORIAN & EDWARDIAN LOCOMOTIVES

David Baxter

MPC

British Library Cataloguing in Publication
Data

Baxter, David, *1928-*
    Victorian & Edwardian locomotives.
    1. Locomotives — Great Britain — History
    1. Title
    625.2′6′0941   TJ603.4.G7

ISBN 0 86190 169 X

Published by
Moorland Publishing Co Ltd,
8 Station Street,
Ashbourne, Derbyshire,
DE6 1DE England.
Tel: (0335) 44486

Printed in UK by
Butler and Tanner Ltd,
Frome, Somerset.

Contents

Isle of Man

Beyer Peacock built fourteen of these 3ft 0in gauge locomotives for the Isle of
Man Railway between 1873 and 1926, and another one was built for the
Manx Northern which merged with the Isle of Man in 1904. Now simply a
tourist attraction, rather than a means of transport, the Port Erin branch of
the railway is still operated during the summer and no 4 *Loch* is one of the
locomotives still in working order. It was Beyer Peacock no 1416, built in
1874. The rerailing jack is on the top of the tank.

1
Introduction

In the 1830s the steam locomotive, or 'locomotive travelling engine' as it was originally called, came out of a thirty-odd year period of experimentation by the early mechanical engineers, Trevithick, Blenkinsop, Murray, Hedley and Stephenson among others and, with the opening of the commercially successful Liverpool and Manchester Railway, established itself as a practical and economic alternative to horse haulage.

By the 1850s a railway network had spread across the country and continued to expand well into the twentieth century. The railway had become the main mass distribution system and inland transport without which the industrial expansion of Victorian times would not have been possible.

Until the coming of the electric tramcar at the turn of the century, followed a few years later by the increasing availability of the motor car and lorry, the railway engine was, for some seventy years, the only known form of mechanical inland transport.

It naturally created a great deal of interest and a pictorial record of this important phase of industrial development was made possible by another emerging technology, that of photography. This also had a lengthy period of experiment, becoming a practical possibility in 1839 with Daguerre's daguerrotype, which reproduced pictures without a negative on a polished copper plate coated with silver, and Fox-Talbot's negative positive process which he perfected in 1841 as the calotype.

From 1851 Frederick Scott Archer's wet collodion process using glass plates coated with 'collodion', which was a form of gun cotton in ether, gradually replaced the two earlier systems. They had the disadvantage however that the plates had to be developed while still wet, within minutes of the photograph being taken.

In 1867 dry collodion-bromide plates became commercially available but they required very long exposures. In 1879 dry gelatine plates were introduced and the first exposure times of under a second became possible, thus signifying the beginning of modern photography.

The early photographs had to be of stationary objects because of the exposure times and it was some while before cameras with sufficiently fast shutter speeds appeared to permit action shots. Consequently photographs of the Victorian and Edwardian period were usually posed and the photographer still had heavy equipment and plates to carry, so that the photographs have a rather still quality by modern standards.

However those who appreciate their efforts have reason to be grateful to them for preserving a record of their times in which the railway engine played a very significant part.

Finally I should like to record my thanks to Mrs E.L. Shearman for her assistance in the preparation of the ms for this book.

2
Development of the Victorian and Edwardian Locomotive

With the opening in 1830 of the Liverpool and Manchester railway, the first to be operated solely by steam locomotives, the era of mechanical transport began. The new engines were developed and refined in a remarkably short space of time and within a few years had proved themselves to be superior to horse haulage, stationary winding engines and the canals which were the other options on offer. Profits from the Liverpool and Manchester Railway poured in and everyone wanted to promote a railway. By 1844, 2,000 miles of railway had been built, and by 1852 there were 7,500 miles of railway.

One of the most important refinements of the locomotive was the invention in 1841 of Stephenson link motion, first fitted to a North Midland Railway locomotive in September 1842. This utilised a radial link connected at the ends to the two eccentric rods which simplified reversing as well as giving variable cut-off of the cylinder stroke, thus utilising the energy of the steam more efficiently (expansive working). With this the basic two-cylinder design of the locomotive was established for many years to come, although variations in the motion were introduced by some railways, principally to avoid the Stephenson patent.

Apart from the motion, however, there were alternatives of basic concept in locomotive design to be evaluated before a general consensus was achieved. Setting aside some wildly experimental concepts, the main types of locomotive in use in the 1840s and 1850s were:

The Stephenson type
The Bury type
Stephenson long boiler type
The Hackworth type
The Crampton type

The Stephenson type had evolved from the *Rocket* of 1829, the *Planet*, an improved design of 1830 both of which had four wheels; and the *Patentee* of 1833, which was a six-wheel version of the *Planet* which permitted the weight of a larger, more powerful, locomotive to be spread more evenly on the track. Engineers had to tread a difficult path for many years between demands for more powerful locomotives and restrictions on axle loading imposed by lightly-constructed track which tended always to lag behind actual requirements.

The Bury type took its name from Edward Bury, a rival locomotive manufacturer to Robert Stephenson and Co, who adopted a different form of construction which did not, however, easily adapt to a six-wheel form. He used bar frames instead of the plate or 'sandwich' frames of the Stephenson type, larger diameter wheels, inside cylinders and a vertical firebox of D-shape plan with a copper top, nicknamed 'haystack' fireboxes. One of these locomotives is preserved in the National Railway Museum at York, the famous Furness Railway 'copperknob' (albeit somewhat dented in an air raid in 1941). Two Bury type locomotives are illustrated in plates 54 and 55, the second in altered condition.

Bury passionately defended the four-wheel locomotive of his type (2-2-0 single and four-coupled 0-4-0) as being lighter and cheaper. He was appointed locomotive contractor to the London and Birmingham railway which was opened from Euston in 1838 and ultimately provided that company with some forty 0-4-0s and sixty-nine 2-2-0s of his type before resigning in 1846.

Although lighter, the design did not permit of easy extension to six-wheel form due to the difficulty of extending the frames behind the firebox; consequently they could not be increased in power. They served a useful purpose on some early lightly-constructed railways and for this reason found initial favour in America, but the design could not be developed further and on the London and Birmingham railway up to seven locomotives were needed for the heavier goods trains.

The Bury engine did, however, have one advantage over the Stephenson ones; they ran more smoothly and this was partly responsible for the provision of inside frames on the **Stephenson long boiler type** introduced in 1841. The main reason, however, was to increase the boiler length to prevent heat being wasted through the smokebox. There were reports at that time of locomotives going around with red hot smokeboxes! All wheels were placed in front of the firebox as on the Bury type, but fireboxes were square instead of round (plate 48). An outside-cylinder version was introduced in 1843 and single, four-and six-coupled engines were built.

The Hackworth type was evolved by Timothy Hackworth on the Stockton and Darlington railway after he left the employ of George and Robert Stephenson in 1825 to become the locomotive engineer on the S & D. He entered a rival to *Rocket*, the *Sans Pareil*, in the Rainhill trials of 1829, and relations between him and the Stephensons became rather strained. He alone did not favour the multitubular boiler, instead using a single return-flue boiler with the chimney and firebox at the same end; thus the driver and fireman were at opposite ends with a tender at front and rear. Vertical or inclined cylinders were used and his designs were thus somewhat primitive by comparison with the multitubular boiler, which had obvious advantages in providing greater heating surfaces and more efficient steaming, but Hackworth achieved some success on the S & D with single-flue boilers.

However the railway was mainly a coal-hauling one where high speeds were not required (and not even possible as horse haulage was also used until 1833 on the main line and much later on the branches). Although another version of the Hackworth locomotive combined the single flue with the tubular form in the last four feet of the flue and was more conventional in appearance with only one tender, the type was not widely adopted.

One of these locomotives, *Derwent*, built as late as 1845, is preserved at Darlington North Road Museum. Hackworth did, however, adopt the six-coupled form as early as 1827 and in that respect he was in advance of the general trend.

There was a general belief among early locomotive engineers that in order to steady the engine at speed it was essential to keep the centre of gravity low (another factor in the thinking behind the long boiler type) and in 1843 Thomas Crampton patented a design with the single-driving wheels placed behind the boiler with greater boiler efficiency, lower centre of gravity and even larger driving wheels some seven or eight feet in diameter.

The Crampton type engines were capable of high speed and gave a smooth ride. However, this was due to the fact that Crampton was one of the first to appreciate the need for proper balancing of moving parts. This, rather than the centre of gravity was the real reason for the rough riding. The difficulty with his design was to provide sufficient loading of the driving wheels to obtain satisfactory adhesion, and it did not permit coupled wheels. However this type and the long boiler type did find favour in other European countries.

Once the principles of balancing had been understood it was the Stephenson type which formed the basis of the British express passenger engine, a 2-2-2 with the rear axle behind a larger firebox. Double frames were, at first, most popular though inside plate frames became gradually more dominant and inside cylinders became more common than outside. With the 2-2-2 arrangement for passenger engines (plates 13, 18-20, 63, 79, 80, 132-5) the 2-4-0 coupled type was commonly used for goods trains (plates 14, 15, 27, 61).

However, the six-coupled engine, which originated in a Stephenson design of 1833 for the Leicester and Swannington Railway (Stephenson's fourth patent), was constructed in increasing numbers from the 1840s and by the 1870s it had become the standard type for goods engines, as will be seen from the numerous photographs in this book. Although eight-coupled engines (plates 113,119) became available in the 1890s the 0-6-0 remained a popular form right up to the end of steam haulage on British Railways.

Similarly four-coupled passenger engines supplanted the early singles. The 2-4-0 arrangement, but with larger driving wheels for higher speeds, was the most popular (plates 2, 3, 6-8, 21-4, 33, 35-9, 47, 72, 75-6, 81) but the 0-4-2 was also employed for passenger engines on some railways (plates 34, 59, 137) with some success.

Before about 1870 cabs were not provided on locomotives (plates 4, 14, 15, 18, 21, 23, 31, 33, 66, 75, 76) but increasing train speeds led to the introduction of weatherboards, sometimes bent rearward at the top (plates 18, 31, 33) to give some protection from the elements. When cabs began to be provided opinions were at first divided between engineers and enginemen as to the amount of protection needed. Many of the older drivers opposed their introduction as restricting their lines of vision. Some companies such as the Midland, London and North Western, Great Northern and Great Western initially provided 'half cabs' covering only half of the footplate, but on the Lancashire and Yorkshire Railway, and the North Eastern Railway large overall cabs were provided from the 1880s. Existing locomotives had cabs of the various types fitted to them at this time.

Until the 1860s tank engines were a rarity, almost all engines having tenders. Archibald Sturrock of the Great Northern Railway introduced steam tenders in 1865 and some were also supplied to the Manchester, Sheffield and Lincolnshire Railway (later Great Central Railway) and Caledonian Railway. These were auxiliary engines mounted under the tenders, but they were not particularly successful and were disliked by enginemen.

Tank engines began to be built from the 1860s and in increasing numbers from the 1870s to serve the growing number of branch lines and expanding suburban traffic in and around the large cities. To meet the new demand many companies also rebuilt their older tender engines as tank engines (plate 16). At first most were well tanks (plates 1, 5, 57, 71) with the tanks below the boilers or as saddle tanks above the boiler, but side tank engines mostly became more popular and some of these were also built for the shorter distance express trains (plate 98).

The increasing size of passenger engines led to the 4-4-0 arrangement gradually replacing the 2-4-0. One of the earliest of these is illustrated on the Stockton and Darlington Railway (plate 66) but Sir Daniel Gooch had built ten some five years earlier for the Great Western broad gauge (*Lalla Rookh* class). These, however, had a fixed wheelbase. He had already used the 4-2-2 arrangement for the *Iron Duke* class of 1847–55, renewed in 1871-8 (plate 77). The fixed wheelbase was less critical on the broad gauge but on the standard gauge it was found necessary to provide bogies.

Bogie locomotives had been built for the USA as early as 1835 and these became standard there in the 1840s. Some American-built 4-2-0s were obtained by the Birmingham and Gloucester Railway in 1847, which were a development of the Bury type. James Pearson had used bogies for an unusual 4-2-4 tank engine design on the broad gauge Bristol and Exeter Railway in 1853 and for a 4-4-0 tank engine of 1855. Alexander McDonnell introduced the swing-link bogie from America to the Great Southern and Western Railway in Ireland in 1877 and in 1884 to the North Eastern Railway. William Adams, however, brought out his design of radial bogie on the North London Railway in 1865 (plate 30) and it was his design which found most favour.

The 4-4-0 ultimately became as much a standard for passenger locomotives as the 0-6-0 for goods and many illustrations are included.

Increasing train speeds and weights necessitated improved braking on trains. This was prompted by public and parliamentary concern over numerous accidents caused by trains running away out of control and in the 1870s many different types of brake were experimented with.

The Midland Railway arranged with the Royal Commission on railway accidents, then sitting, to hold trials on the Nottingham to Newark line in June 1875 and in addition to four Midland trains others from the Great

Northern, Caledonian, London and North Western, Lancashire and Yorkshire and London, Brighton and South Coast railways also took part. The brakes tested were Clarke and Webb's chain brake (L & NW), Smith's non-automatic (GN), automatic reaction (Caledonian), Fry's mechanical (L & Y) and Westinghouse automatic air brake (Midland and LBSC) the latter being the most successful.

In 1876-8 the Great Western carried out trials with Sanders automatic vacuum brake and, with some improvements, the automatic vacuum brake was adopted by most railways including the Midland although some adopted the Westinghouse and many locomotives were equipped for both systems for interworking of stock (plate 7). A common arrangement was for steam brakes on the engine and vacuum brakes on the train controlled from the footplate — a vast improvement on the old hand braking of trains used in earlier days. The Regulation of Railways Act 1889 made mandatory continuous brakes on passenger trains, interlocking of points and signals and the block system (offer and acceptance of trains by each signalman one at a time).

An important development in the last quarter of the nineteenth century was the introduction on the London and North Western and the North Eastern railways of large numbers of compound engines (L & NW plate 25) and other railways also built experimental compounds with the object of achieving economy, but the results were not overwhelmingly successful. Further details of the Webb divided-drive system on the London and North Western Railway and the Worsdell von Bories system on the North Eastern Railway are given under those company's respective headings. In 1898 W.M. Smith of the North Eastern Railway perfected a three-cylinder system which was adopted by Samuel Johnson of the Midland Railway in 1902 and further improved by Richard Deeley. This used one high-pressure cylinder and two low-pressure ones. Compounds were also built by the Great Central Railway (plate 70). The French de Glehn four-cylinder system with two high-pressure and two low-pressure cylinders was tried by the Great Western Railway in 1903-5.

However development in Britain of modern valve gear (W.M. Smith of the NER also perfected the piston valve, an improvement on the slide valve) produced thermal efficiency with a single stage of expansion that was equal to the compounds and after 1910 superheating was increasingly used instead.

In the latter part of the nineteenth century larger locomotives with bigger boilers began to make their appearance. The introduction of steam sanding brought about a revival of singles on the Midland Railway (plates 9, 10), North Eastern Railway (all being compounds), Great Central and Great Eastern railways with the 4-2-2 arrangement to accommodate the larger boiler. On the Great Northern Railway Patrick Stirling and Henry A. Ivatt built sixty-five 4-2-2s between 1870 and 1901 as well as smaller 2-2-2s and Stirling's number 1 8ft single of 1870 can be seen in the National Railway Museum at York. The Great Western Railway built 2-2-2s and 4-2-2s in the 1890s (plate 88, 89), the former being later converted to 4-2-2s.

On several railways the 4-4-2 'Atlantic' arrangement was used (Great

Central plate 70) and some tank engine 'Atlantics' were also built (Great Western plate 98).

The North Eastern Railway was the first to use the 4-6-0 for passenger trains in 1899 although David Jones of the Highland railway had introduced some for goods working in 1894, one of which is now in the Glasgow Transport Museum. The 4-6-0 arrangement found general favour from the Edwardian period onwards (Great Western plates 94-6), many having three or four cylinders.

For heavier freight and shunting work eight-coupled tank and tender engines were introduced (plate 119) and the first use of these was on the Barry railway in 1889 (plate 113).

There were some twenty thousand locomotives in use on the railways of Britain in 1900, not to mention many more in service in industry and around the world which had been built in Britain. By 1910 there were still, despite many amalgamations, nearly one hundred locomotive-owning railways on the British mainland, twenty-two of which owned more than a hundred locomotives plus a further six small companies in the Isle of Man (frontispiece), Isle of Wight and Jersey. In Ireland there were six major trunk routes plus a number of minor and narrow gauge railways.

All of them kept their locomotives in immaculate condition. Every locomotive whatever its duty was brightly polished and spotlessly clean. Different economic conditions permitted a high level of employment to make this possible and railway workers enjoyed a good social status and steady employment. As can be seen from the photographs they took an immense pride in their work.

In 1904 the Great Western 4-4-0 *City of Truro* (now in the Swindon Railway Museum) (*City* class plate 91) had exceeded 100mph for the first time and at the close of Edward VII's reign the railways were at their apogee. Ahead lay further technical developments with even larger locomotives and many fine achievements, but also two world wars and increasing competition from road transport both public and private.

The age of steam's supremacy was over.

3
Midland Railway

The company was formed in 1844 by the amalgamation of three smaller ones centred on Derby. The Midland Counties Railway connected with the London and Birmingham railway at Rugby and the Birmingham and Derby Junction railway connected with the L & B at Hampton-in-Arden. The third company, the North Midland Railway, ran north from Derby to Leeds and was eventually connected with the North Eastern and North British railways providing a circuitous route from London Euston, soon shortened by the more direct Great Northern Railway south of Leeds.

The Midland Railway acquired the two companies operating the Birmingham to Bristol line in 1847 and converted the Gloucester to Bristol section from broad gauge to standard gauge — a defeat for the Great Western. It extended into London and opened its own London terminus, St Pancras in 1868. The main line was completed with the opening in 1876 of the now famous Settle to Carlisle line, a prodigious feat of engineering requiring equally prodigious skill in operating it, especially in winter. Services also ran to Liverpool (Central) and Manchester (Central).

Its first locomotive engineer was Matthew Kirtley and during the twenty-nine years he was in charge the locomotive stock increased by over ten fold. So well built were the locomotives he designed that many of them were still in use when the railways were nationalised in 1948. A former pupil of the Stephenson's, Kirtley was instrumental in 1859 in introducing a brick arch in the firebox, usually combined with a baffle plate to deflect the flames through a longer path before reaching the tubes. This facilitated the burning of coal sufficiently smokelessly to satisfy statutory requirements. Because of these requirements all the early locomotives burned coke which was much more expensive.

The Midland Railway throughout its existence adhered to a small-engine policy, preferring to double head or to run extra trains. It never had six-coupled passenger engines or eight-coupled goods engines, but it did have large numbers of 0-6-0s for the heavy mineral traffic that it carried.

Express passenger trains over the Settle to Carlisle line were originally operated by the 2-4-0 800 and 890 classes (plates 6, 7, 8) and the later 1070 class and were then worked forward to Glasgow and Edinburgh by the Glasgow and South Western and North British railways respectively.

Kirtley was succeeded in 1873 by Samuel Waite Johnson. His first designs were based on Kirtley's specifications but he switched from outside to inside frames. Johnson is well known for the graceful lines he introduced into his designs particularly in the five classes of 4-2-2 which he introduced between 1887 and 1900, two of which are illustrated (plates 9, 10). He also changed the locomotive colour from green to red. He introduced the 4-4-0 on the Midland (plates 11, 12) which ultimately became the standard Midland main line passenger engine and in 1902 on his last 4-4-0 class he adopted the Smith system of three-cylinder compounding, later further improved by Richard Deeley.

1 MR 5 class

Originally built in 1855, jointly by the Midland Railway and the firm of E.B. Wilson and Co of Leeds, this 0-6-0 well tank locomotive was originally a 2-2-2 of 5 class which was itself a somewhat hybrid batch of engines utilising parts from even earlier ones which had been withdrawn. Most of these had only a short life, being broken up in the 1860s, but some, including 214, were rebuilt as tank engines and completely renewed. No 214 was made a saddle tank locomotive in 1872 and became a well tank locomotive in 1876; the photograph shows it as it was in the period 1876-89. Originally numbered 16 as a 2-2-2, the locomotive was renumbered many times, 214 being, in fact, the sixth number carried. It was broken up in June 1898.

2 MR 156 class

This 2-4-0 was one of Matthew Kirtley's 156 class, no 104, dating from April 1867. Originally it had a smaller boiler with raised firebox and only a sloping weatherboard instead of a cab. In 1879 it was transferred to the duplicate list being replaced by a new 104 and 'written off' in the company's accounts as an asset; on the MR this was signified by adding the letter A to the number. Nonetheless, 104A still had a long useful life ahead. Renumbered 6 in 1907 when the duplicate list numbering was abolished on the MR, it survived to become LMS no 6 in 1923 and was not withdrawn until December 1932. The photograph shows the engine as it appeared in the period 1882-1907.

3 MR 156 class

No 106A was also of 156 class dating from June 1867 and is seen here in the same period as 104A, although it was rebuilt to this condition with new boiler and cab one year earlier than 104A in 1881. It went to the duplicate list in the same month (June 1879). It was renumbered 8 in 1907 and became LMS 8 in 1923, having an even longer life than no 6, not being withdrawn until June 1942. From 1935 it was used for officer's special inspection trains on the former LNWR lines of the LMS, at first in the Liverpool area and then at Watford and from 1937 at Walsall.

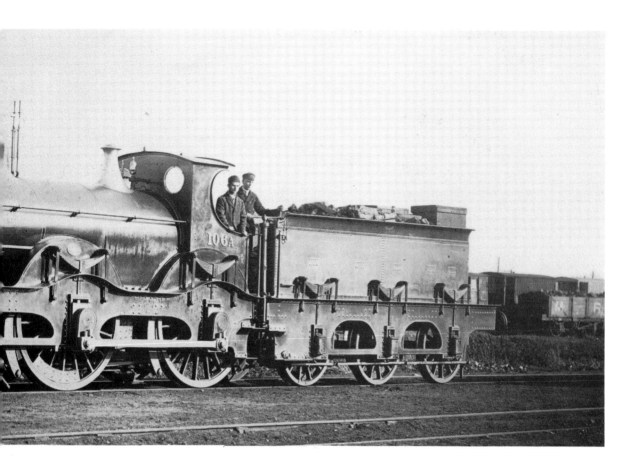

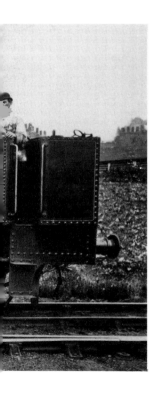

4   204 class

With the opening of St Pancras station in London in 1868, a connection was provided for through city-bound passenger trains to the Moorgate area over the Metropolitan Railway, now part of the Circle Line of London Transport. This was then, of course, steam operated and because, as now, the stations were underground, locomotives had to condense their smoke in the water tanks. The MR had ordered ten 2-4-0Ts from the firm of Beyer Peacock in Manchester to work the service, but they proved to have too rigid a wheelbase and arrangements were made with the Metropolitan to divert six 4-4-0Ts being built by Beyer Peacock for the Metropolitan to the MR. Numbered 204-9, 205 was delivered in September 1868 and was Beyer Peacock works number 776. It is shown in original condition before rebuilding in 1888. Cabs were added in 1900/1. No 205 was withdrawn in 1908 as no 1199. Note the condenser (long horizontal pipe) and short wheelbase bogie (Bissel truck).

5 MR 202

This small well tank engine was originally built in June 1852 by William Fairbairn and Sons who had a works in Canal Street, Manchester. It was built originally as a 2–2–2 well tank engine for the North Western Railway which ran from Skipton to Lancaster and was often known as the 'Little North Western' to distinguish it from the much larger London and North Western Railway. On 1 January 1871, the NWR was absorbed by the Midland Railway, who had previously entered into an agreement to work the line, taking over the locomotives and stock on 1 June 1852. On the North Western no 202 had originally been named *Competitor* but the MR removed the name and renumbered it 159. In January 1865 it was rebuilt as an 0–4–2 well tank locomotive and became no 202 in May 1866. It was renumbered again several times and was broken up as 2065A in October 1892.

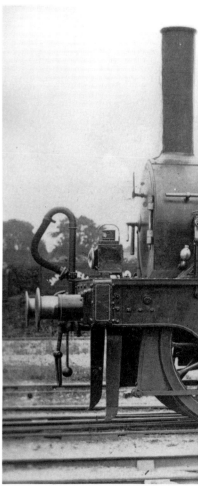

6 MR 800 class

This was one of Kirtley's most famous classes, the 800 class built for express passenger trains, including those over the newly-opened Settle to Carlisle line. When they were built only weatherboards were provided, and no 61, which was built at Derby works in April 1870, is here seen after rebuilding by Kirtley's successor S.W. Johnson in 1882 with new boiler and a cab. It was transferred to the duplicate list as 61A in 1898 and became no 29 in the general renumbering of 1907. In 1923 it became LMS 29 and was withdrawn in November 1925. The driving wheels were 6ft 8in diameter.

8 MR 890 class

These were similar to the 800 class but were built later with boilers eleven inches shorter and one inch smaller in diameter. In fact Matthew Kirtley died in office while they were being completed and the last thirty were finished at Derby after his death. No 78 was one of these, built in November 1874. The photograph was taken in Nottingham when the locomotive was brand new. In April 1889 it was rebuilt with a Johnson boiler. At the same time the cylinders were enlarged from 17×24in to 18×24in. Note the elaborate burnishing of the frames and leading splasher. Young lads aspiring to be enginemen had to start as cleaners and many had their own distinctive patterns for this burnishing. No 78 became 115 in 1907 and LMS 115 in 1923 (class 1P) being withdrawn in February 1937.

7 MR 800 class

This 2-4-0 was of the same class as no 61, 800 class, but was one of six built at Derby in 1871, which varied from the 1870 locomotives in having the coupled wheelbase three inches shorter. The photograph shows no 22 (built in October 1871) after rebuilding in December 1875 with Johnson boiler and cab. As will be seen, however, the original open splashers have still been retained at this stage whereas no 61 has had the splashers filled in. No 22 was again rebuilt in 1889 when its appearance would be as no 61. From about 1880 some locomotives of 800 class — those working to Carlisle — were fitted with Westinghouse air compressors in addition to vacuum brakes. These locomotives were used with North British through carriages, which were fitted with Westinghouse brakes, travelling to Edinburgh Waverley. No 22 was one of these, the Westinghouse pump being seen on the side of the boiler. It became no 66 in 1907 and was withdrawn in September 1911.

9 MR 1853 class

The 1853 class was the second of five classes of singles designed by Johnson between 1887 and 1900. The invention of steam sanding produced a revival of single driving wheel locomotives after many years. They were thought by many to be the most graceful locomotives ever designed and were often called 'Spinners' due to their smooth silent running. With no coupling rods to dismantle for repairs they were also looked on favourably by fitters. Driving wheel sizes varied from 7ft 4in to 7ft 9½in. The 1853 class had 7ft 6in driving wheels. No 1864 was built at Derby to order no 809 in 1889 and was renumbered 621 in 1907, being withdrawn in November 1921.

12 2606 class
No 2608 was one of Johnson's 2606 class built at Derby to order no 1869 in 1900. The photograph shows it as built with bogie tender. Later they were reboilered with extended smoke boxes, and the original tenders, which held 4,000 gallons of water, were replaced with smaller six-wheel ones. In 1907 no 2608 became 702 of 700 class and LMS 702 3P class in 1923. It was withdrawn in November 1931.

10 MR 115 class

No 115 was the first of a later class of 4–2–2s with larger cylinders, $19\frac{1}{2} \times 26$in as against 18in, $18\frac{1}{2}$in and 19in on the earlier classes. Driving wheels were 7ft 9in. No 115 was built at Derby to order no 1474 in November 1896. In 1907 it became no 670, and LMS 670 in 1923, being withdrawn in January 1926. Another locomotive of this class, no 118, was preserved and has been restored to its 1907 condition as no 672 in working order by the Midland Railway Trust. It may be seen at its preservation site at Butterley in Derbyshire. This photograph shows no 115, almost certainly outside St Pancras station near the very prominent gas holder.

11 MR 156 class

This was probably an official photograph of no 156 which was the first of a class of 4–4–0s brought out by Johnson in 1896. Twenty-five were built at Derby between then and 1901 and a further twenty were built by Sharp Stewart and Co in 1889. No 156 was built to order no 1458 and was renumbered 423 in 1907. In common with all the others of the class, Sir Henry Fowler completely renewed it in 1918 as 483 class with much larger boiler. This very much altered the appearance, but in this condition, as LMS 2P no 423, it survived to become BR 40423 and was withdrawn in August 1952.

4
London & North Western
and
North London Railways

Before 1923 the L & NW was the largest railway in Britain. Its main line was the West Coast Route from Euston to Carlisle whence through trains to Scotland were worked forward by the Caledonian Railway. From Crewe there were lines to Holyhead, Manchester (London Road) and Liverpool (Lime Street) and from Chester to Manchester (Exchange), Huddersfield and Leeds. It had a network of lines centred on Birmingham (New Street), which was a joint station with the Midland Railway and the Central Wales line to Swansea from Shrewsbury. There were many branch lines in the Midlands and in North West England.

The London and North Western Railway was formed in 1846 by the amalgamation of the London and Birmingham, Grand Junction and Manchester and Birmingham railways (the latter ran over the GJR line from Crewe). These companies all had their own locomotive works and initially they continued to function with their own locomotive policies as separate divisions. The GJR had already absorbed the Liverpool and Manchester railway and set up Crewe works in 1843. These became the works of the Northern Division of the L & NW and the former engineer of the GJR Francis Trevithick became the first Northern Division engineer.

He was the eldest son of the pioneer locomotive engineer Richard Trevithick who built the first ever experimental steam railway locomotive in 1803 (to which he referred as a 'tram-waggon'). Francis Trevithick's main claim to fame was the original design of the 2-2-2 *Cornwall* in which he tried to go one better than Crampton by placing the boiler below the driving axle. Not very surprisingly it was not a success and was rebuilt in conventional form (plate 13). The name was no doubt chosen because he came from a Cornish family.

Trevithick had a very able assistant and works manager, Alexander Allan, who made a much more lasting impression on locomotive development. Allan, a Scot from Montrose, had been with Robert Stephenson and Co at the time when *Patentee* was being developed, and he designed a version of the Stephenson type of locomotive with outside cylinders and double frames; singles for passenger engines and 2-4-0s for goods (plates 14, 15) which became known as the 'Crewe type'.

In 1853 Allan was appointed locomotive engineer for the Scottish Central railway, which became part of the Caledonian, and introduced the Crewe type there. It was subsequently adopted on several other railways in this country (plate 61) and abroad.

In 1854 he patented a variation of the Stephenson link motion which he had developed at Crewe known as Allan straight link motion in which the reversing lever raised the valve rod at the same time as it lowered the eccentric rods and link. On the Stephenson motion the link was curved.

The Manchester and Birmingham Railway had a works at Longsight in Manchester which became the L & NW North Eastern Division works. In 1857 it was decided to merge the NE Division with the Northern Division and close the works at Longsight. The engineer in charge of these works was John Ramsbottom and he was appointed to take charge at Crewe in preference to Trevithick, who resigned.

From 1862 Ramsbottom became the locomotive engineer for the whole of the L & NW, and he has been described as the father of the modern locomotive. His contributions to mechanical engineering are indeed numerous. In 1850 he perfected a double-beat regulator valve. In 1852 he invented the split piston ring of rolled brass in place of the hemp packing which had sufficed until then. Improved still further by David Joy in 1855, such piston rings have been used ever since in all piston engines, whether steam or internal combustion. In 1856 Ramsbottom designed a safety valve which was almost universally used for the next sixty years or so, and in the same year he introduced a displacement lubricator.

The first locomotives built by him at Crewe were the DX goods (plate 17) of which some 860 were eventually built, the largest single class of locomotives at that time. His 2-4-0 designs (plates 21, 22, 23) were equally successful but the *Problem* 2-2-2 class (plates 19,20) were probably the most celebrated for their part in the London to Scotland 'races' against the East Coast competition. He also introduced standardisation of parts at Crewe and in 1860 devised the first water pick-up apparatus.

The engineer in charge at the Wolverton works of the Southern Division, until his resignation in 1862, was James Edward McConnell, who had succeeded Edward Bury in 1847. The works were originally sited at Wolverton by the London and Birmingham railway as being half-way between the two cities.

As can be seen, McConnell's designs (plate 18) were quite different from the Northern Division locomotives and they were painted brick red in contrast to the Northern Division black. His three classes of 'bloomers' were his most celebrated designs. Bloomers were knickerbocker trousers for women introduced by Mrs Amelia Bloomer and the nickname may have been adopted because of the high running plates on the locomotives.

Francis William Webb, who succeeded Ramsbottom, had previously been his assistant and his first designs were a continuation of Ramsbottom's (plate 24). He later modernised many of the Ramsbottom locomotives as *Renewed Precedent* class and *Special DX*, in which form many were still running in the 1950s. The *Precedents* became as celebrated as the *Problem* (or *Lady of the Lake*) class.

However Webb is now principally remembered for his persistent devotion to compounding. His five classes of divided-drive three-cylinder compounds had two outside high-pressure cylinders and one low-pressure cylinder inside the frame. The divided drive was intended to produce the effect of two single engines working in tandem but they were unreliable in practice and had starting difficulties which could result, if the engine had reversed on to the train, in the wheels slipping in opposite directions. The second of these classes, the *Dreadnought* class is illustrated in plate 25. The last two classes with divided drive were much larger with very long boilers and an additional pair of trailing wheels. Webb later switched to 4-4-0 coupled four-cylinder compounds for passenger working and eight-coupled locomotives for goods. His 'coal tank' engine (plate 26) was a tank engine version of his 'coal' 0-6-0s, a very successful development of the DX goods.

Webb was an autocratic man, who never married and had few friends, but he enjoyed the confidence of L & NW Chairman Sir Richard Moon. However after his eventual retirement in 1904 his successor, George Whale, lost no time in completely eliminating compound working from the L & NW.

North London Railway

This railway was closely associated with the L & NW and the first locomotive engineer at their works at Bow in London was William Adams. The railway had somewhat specialised traffic and the locomotives were suited to particular needs. For suburban passenger traffic Adams designed the 4-4-0 tank with his design of radial bogie (plate 30).

Adams went to the Great Eastern Railway in 1873, and the London and South Western Railway in 1878, where he achieved most distinction as a locomotive designer (plate 128, 129).

John Carter Park replaced Adams and designed the 0-6-0 tank engine (plates 28, 29) for goods working. One of these is now on the Bluebell Railway in Sussex. With short haulage distances the NLR latterly relied entirely on tank engines.

13 LNW *Cornwall*

A very famous locomotive with a long history. Originally built in 1847 in a
different form, with the boiler underslung beneath the driving axle. This was
possible because of the large 8ft 6in driving wheel, the idea being to keep the
centre of gravity low. It was rebuilt the following year as a 4-2-2, and in this
form was exhibited at the Great Exhibition in 1851. In November 1858 it was
completely renewed with conventional boiler mounting as seen here, the cab
being added about twenty years later. Originally numbered 173, it went to
the duplicate list as 3020 in June 1886 and from March 1913 was used for
hauling an officer's inspection saloon. It was exhibited at the Darlington
Centenary in 1925 and was restored at Crewe works in 1933. It is now in the
National Railway Museum collection, York.

15 LNW LFB Goods

This was also an LFB Goods engine of the same class as 137, built in
September 1854 as Crewe works number 305. It originally carried the name
Warrior, which was not removed until February 1872. This photograph
therefore dates from the period 1872–80 when the locomotive was transferred
to duplicate list as no 1923 and was broken up in August 1883. Note that the
LNW was still using painted numbers at this period instead of the plates used
on later engines.

27

14 LNW LFB Goods

Built at Crewe in May 1853, this 2-4-0 was of the LFB (large firebox) goods type engine and was originally named *Crane*. It was one of a group of passenger singles and four-coupled goods engines known generally as the 'Crewe types' being designed by Alexander Allan and Francis Trevithick at Crewe. The basic design with modifications was subsequently adopted on many other railways. The photograph shows the engine in the period 1862–80 after names had been removed from the goods engines. In 1880 it went to the duplicate list as no 1962 and was cut up in February 1883.

17 LNW DX Goods

John Ramsbottom, described by some as the father of the modern locomotive, who invented the piston ring in 1852 (still in use on modern internal combustion engines) amongst other things, designed this goods engine in 1858 and over 900 were eventually built. They were known as the DX type, a term relating to a system used in Crewe works to denote order batches. No 1025 was a fairly early example, being built in August 1862 (Crewe works number 560). It is seen here after rebuilding in 1873, with Webb cab added, but it still retains the Ramsbottom smoke-box with sloping front. It was placed on the duplicate list as no 1882 in May 1887, renumbered 3339 in November 1898 and withdrawn in April 1899.

16 LNW Rebuilt LFB Goods

This locomotive started life as an LFB goods engine built in March 1856 and named *Cuckoo* (Crewe works number 360). In September 1876 it was rebuilt as a 2-4-0 saddle tank locomotive and given a number plate as seen here. The name had already been removed in May 1872. As will be seen by comparing this with the photographs of unrebuilt goods type engines, the frames, wheels and cylinders are unchanged but in addition to the saddle tank it has a new Webb-type chimney and dome and, of course, a bunker has been added for coal in place of the tender. The side plate has also been replaced. In this condition it would be used for shunting and short haul local goods trains. It went to duplicate list in September 1884 as no 1861 and was broken up in July 1886.

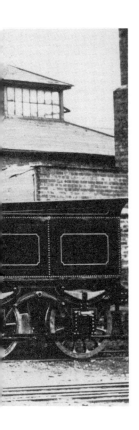

18 LNW (Southern Division) Small 'bloomer'

Until 1862 the Southern Division of the LNW was managed separately under its own locomotive engineer, J.E McConnell, and the engines were numbered in their own sequence. No 381 was built at the Southern Division locomotive works at Wolverton, which later became the carriage works, as it still is today. The engine was built in October 1861, and it was originally named *Councillor*. It was the last of a class of 6ft 6in singles nicknamed small 'bloomers'. Bloomers were a fashionable form of ladies underwear at the time although the connection between these and the locomotives is not now too clear. Large 'bloomers' had 7ft driving wheels and both were to McConnell's design. The photograph was probably taken at Wolverton works, which were originally built by the London and Birmingham Railway. It became LNW 981 in May 1862. It was cut up in December 1883. Note the number on the front of the chimney.

19 LNW *Problem*

At the same period Ramsbottom designed this single-driving wheel passenger locomotive, which achieved fame as the *Problem* or *Lady of the Lake* class, built during 1859–65. No 610 was built at Crewe works (works number 590) in December 1862. Webb cabs were added in the 1870s. These graceful locomotives were used in the London to Edinburgh 'races' of 1888 between East and West coast routes. Webb modernised them with larger boilers in the late 1890s, and *Princess Royal* received this rebuilding in March 1899. Train weights by then, however, were becoming too heavy for them and all were withdrawn by 1907, no 610 in February 1905. The driving wheels were 7ft 7½in diameter.

20 LNW *Problem*

This photograph can be dated exactly to June 1873, when no 806 *Waverley* was temporarily renamed *Nasir al Din* in Arabic in honour of the State visit of the Shah of Persia. In addition, as can be seen, it carried a replica of the crown on the boiler for the occasion. The locomotive was *Problem* class built in February 1863 to Crewe works number 598, and as will be noted, it had already been provided with a cab, but the splashers are still open. It was rebuilt in November 1895 and was cut up in January 1905.

21 LNW *Samson*

This was the Ramsbottom *Samson* class with 6ft 1½in driving wheels, the first four-coupled passenger engines on the LNWR. No 742 *Spitfire* was built at Crewe in July 1864 (works number 735). They were officially described as 'Curved Link 6ft Passenger' locomotives and were intended for mixed traffic duties. This photograph shows the engine as originally designed by Ramsbottom. Cabs were added in the 1870s, so the photograph was certainly taken before 1873. The driver has his hand on the regulator. The man in the bowler hat, who may have been an inspector, is holding the tender brake wheel. There were no brakes on the engine but counter-pressure braking was used by screwing the reversing wheel into reverse gear and opening the regulator slightly. *Spitfire* was withdrawn in December 1892.

22 LNW *Newton*

Newton class locomotives were larger than those of the *Samson* class, with 6ft
7½in driving wheels and larger boilers. The cabs were added in the 1870s
and the splashers later filled in. *Abercrombie* is seen here with cab but with the
splashers still open as built. The photograph can thus be dated to about
1873–5. No 1525 was built in November 1866 (Crewe number 992). All of the
class were renewed, (ie very extensively rebuilt and regarded as new engines)
from 1887 by Webb, then being classed as Renewed (or Improved) *Precedent*
class. No 1525 was renewed in May 1891.

24 LNW *Samson*

Francis W. Webb took over as locomotive superintendent from Ramsbottom in 1871, but the first passenger engines turned out from Crewe works under his control were to the Ramsbottom design, being forty more *Samson* class of which no 631 *Hotspur* was one. Built in October 1874, it was Crewe works number 1848. However, all of these were fitted with cabs when new. Note the shorter coupled wheelbase of 7ft 2in compared with 8ft 3in on the *Newton* class. *Hotspur* was not rebuilt, being put on the duplicate list as no 3273 in January 1896, and in November 1901 was renamed *Engineer Manchester* for hauling the Manchester District engineer's saloon. It was withdrawn in June 1914.

23 LNW *Newton*

No 2004 *Witch* was of the same class as no 1525, but is seen here in original condition as built without a cab. It will be noticed that the handrail along the boiler to which one of the two boys is holding is lower than on the later photograph of no 1525. The boys, probably about 12 or 13, were almost certainly cleaners (the one on the running plate has his cleaning rag in his hand), and it was probably a very proud moment for them. Note the screw reversing wheel clearly visible on the footplate. No 2004 was in the last batch of *Newton* class locomotives to be built in April 1871. It was Crewe works number 1383 and it was renewed as Improved *Precedent* class in May 1891.

25 LNW *Dreadnought*

No 173 *City of Manchester* was of the *Dreadnought* class, built in March 1886 at Crewe (works number 2896). This class was the second of Webb's divided drive compound classes of which there were five. The driving wheels were not coupled and were, in effect, two single-drive engines working in tandem, two outside high-pressure cylinders driving the rear wheels and one inside low-pressure cylinder driving the leading driving wheels. They put up some good running at speed, but often had difficulty starting. After Webb retired in 1903 his successor, George Whale, lost no time in having them cut up, no 173 in August 1904.

27 LNW ex-St Helens Canal and Railway

This locomotive was originally built by the St Helens Canal and Railway at St Helens, Lancashire in 1863 as their number 21 named *White Raven*. It was originally a 2-4-2 tank engine but was altered to 2-4-0 soon after being built, although the exact date is not known. It became LNW 1387 in July 1864 when the LNW took over the St Helens railway, and was transferred to the duplicate list as no 1226 in December 1867 and renumbered 1818, as seen here in December 1871. Again renumbered 3040 in November 1886, it was scrapped in July 1888.

26 LNW Coal Tank

These Webb 0-6-2 tank engines were known as coal tanks, being a tank version of the 0-6-0 coal engines with 17×24in cylinders and 4ft $5\frac{1}{2}$in driving wheels (4ft 3in nominal excluding tyre thickness). They were distinct from the 18in tank engines which had 18×24in cylinders and driving wheels 9in larger. Although the 18in tank engines were specifically designed for passenger working, the coal tank locomotives were fitted with vacuum brakes and were frequently used on local passenger trains, as here. The station is in the Manchester area, possibly Longsight or Levenshulme. No 2360 was Crewe works number 2866 of April 1886. It became LMS 7724 although the number was not applied until February 1928 and was withdrawn in August 1938.

28 LNW ex-North London Railway

This 0-6-0 tank engine was designed by J.C. Park for goods trains on the North London Railway, which was taken over by the LNWR in 1922 but which had been managed by them since 1 January 1909. Twelve locomotives had on that date been transferred to the LNW. No 2631 was one of them, having been built in 1882 at the North London locomotive works at Bow. It became LMS 7507, this number being applied in May 1927. The original North London number was 79. It was scrapped in December 1932. The North London Railway connected with the LNWR at Chalk Farm.

29 North London goods tank

The North London Railway worked in close conjunction with the LNWR, as all the LNW traffic to and from London docks travelled over it. These 0-6-0 tank engines were used for working goods trains and no 61, built at Bow works by the NLR in 1895, was a modernisation of a design first introduced by J.C. Park in 1879. Extensively rebuilt (officially 'renewed') in 1901, no 61 became LNW 2879 in 1922 and in September 1926 was renumbered LMS 7524. In September 1934 it was again renumbered 27524 and was withdrawn in March 1936.

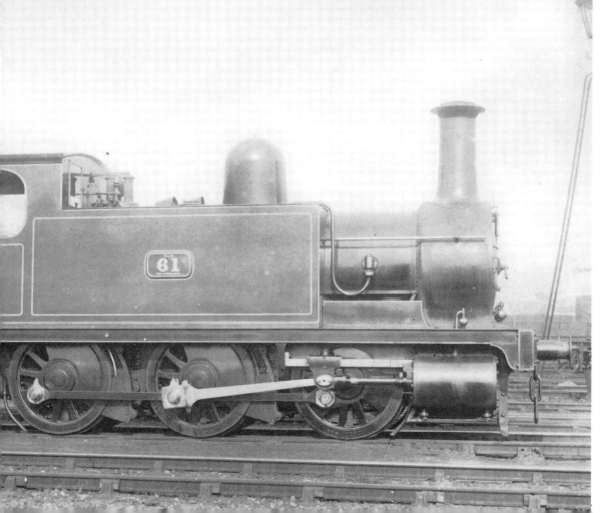

30 North London passenger tank

The NLR also had an intensive passenger service into their city terminus at Broad Street from north London and Richmond, for which these 4-4-0 tanks were used. They were based on an original design of William Adams, Park's predecessor, in 1861. No 48 was a renewal of an earlier no 48, and was built in 1899 at Bow works. In 1922 when the LNW took over the line, it became LNW no 2841 and a year later when the LMS was formed, it was allotted no 6476. However, it was broken up in January 1926 and never actually carried this number. Note the destination board on the front buffer beam. The NLR had through services over several of the main line railways serving London.

5
Lancashire & Yorkshire Railway

The Manchester and Leeds Railway (plates 54, 55) amalgamated with the Manchester and Bolton Railway in 1847 and changed its name to the Lancashire and Yorkshire Railway. It absorbed the Blackburn, Darwen and Bolton Railway in 1850 and the Liverpool, Crosby and Southport in 1855, having extended to Liverpool in 1850. The original route to Leeds via Normanton and the North Midland Railway was replaced by its own route via Halifax and Bradford thence via the Great Northern Railway in the same year.

In 1859 the East Lancashire Railway was incorporated, but operated as a separate division until 1875. It was centred on Bury near Manchester and had sixty-six locomotives (plates 47, 48), many built at Bury. Locomotives built for the East Lancashire Division were standard L & Y types but the ELR practice of naming locomotives was continued (plates 49-53).

The L & Y ultimately extended from Goole in the east to Liverpool, Southport and Blackpool in the west and had a dense network of lines in between. It operated through trains to Newcastle via the North Eastern railway.

In the mid-nineteenth century the railway suffered from indifferent management. Its first locomotive engineer, William Jenkins, set up its own locomotive works at Miles Platting in Manchester in 1846 and began building its own locomotives (plates 32, 33) but locomotive policy was somewhat hand-to-mouth and Great Northern and London and North Western types were also obtained (plates 34, 39) during the period of his successor, William Yates. Lack of investment by the company had resulted in many old locomotives being kept in service too long. Production of the 4 class 2-4-0s (plates 35-7) and the 32 class 2-4-0 tanks (plate 52) did however continue as did the 0-6-0 saddle tanks (plates 40, 53) and some old locomotives were rebuilt (plate 38).

In 1875, in a determined effort to improve the locomotive stock a new locomotive superintendent, William Barton Wright, was appointed and Yates continued as works manager under him until 1886. Barton Wright completely renewed the locomotive stock, purchasing most of the new engines from reliable outside manufacturers (plate 41).

In 1883 John Ramsbottom, now retired from the L & NW, was appointed as a consultant and he advised that a new works should be constructed at an open site. In 1884 land was purchased at Horwich, between Bolton and Chorley, and Barton Wright and Ramsbottom were responsible for planning the new works.

Barton Wright's locomotives, particularly the goods engines, were very long lasting and one 0-6-0 rebuilt as a saddle tank was eighty-seven years old when withdrawn in September 1964. Another of the same class is now on the Keighley and Worth Valley Railway at Haworth.

The former green livery was changed to black on engines in 1879. When the new works was opened in January 1888, Barton Wright had already resigned and Sir John A.F. Aspinall (knighted in 1917) was appointed, a most distinguished engineer who became general manager of the L & Y in 1899.

He introduced new designs of passenger locomotives of 4–4–0 (plates 42-5) and *Atlantic* 4–4–2s as well as express 2–4–2 tanks and later eight-coupled goods engines. Under Aspinall the process of the regeneration of the locomotive stock was completed and the company placed in the forefront of locomotive technology. He also utilised Joy valve gear which was used by Webb on the L & NW railway.

When Aspinall was appointed general manager, Henry Albert Hoy, who had been works manager at Horwich was appointed in his place. He was an innovative engineer and carried out many experiments. Number 1112 of 1093 class (plate 43) was rebuilt in 1901 as a four-cylinder compound with Walschaerts valve gear, but reverted to simple expansion in 1908. Experiments were also carried out with the Druitt Halpin thermal storage apparatus but abandoned about six years later.

Only one class of locomotive was designed by Hoy before he resigned in 1904 to become general manager of Beyer Peacock and Co, to be replaced by George Hughes. This was the 2–6–2 tank engine (plate 46) which, when built, was the largest tank engine in the UK with Belpaire fireboxes and Aspinall vacuum-operated water scoops. They were quite successful on the heavy passenger work for which they were intended but were superseded by smaller superheated tank engines by 1914, after which they were used on goods work.

One of the small companies absorbed by the L & Y was the West Lancashire Railway which ran from Southport to Preston, taken over in 1897. It had acquired second-hand locomotives from the London, Brighton and South Coast Railway but these did not survive long enough to be taken into L & Y stock. One of these is illustrated under LBSC (plate 134) after its sale to the WLR.

32 L & Y Standard goods 303 class

These were of the same period as the 0-4-2 and were the Jenkins standard goods locomotives, built between 1855 and 1870; no 325 in August 1864 (Miles Platting works number 184). In February 1887 it was rebuilt as an 0-6-0 saddle tank engine, with driving wheels reduced from the original 4ft 10in to 4ft 0in. Many other locomotives in the class were rebuilt as tank engines, some being made 0-6-2 tanks and some 0-4-4 tanks. No 325 is seen here after rebuilding with a cab in the 1870s. It was withdrawn in January 1900. Note the old-fashioned 'slotted' signal with the more modern signal arm fixed below it. The 'slotted' arm at the top was probably working in conjunction with the lower one for better sighting from a distance, but has no lights. For the original form of this class, see East Lancashire Division no 62 (plate 49).

31 L & Y 163 class

William Jenkins designed these 0-4-2 locomotives for working goods trains to the specification of J. Hawkshaw, the company's chief engineer in the early days. Hawkshaw was a civil engineer, not a mechanical engineer, and merely stipulated broad requirements for the early locomotive stock, leaving the detailed design work to the Locomotive Superintendent. Thirty-six of these locomotives were built, twenty-six at the L & Y locomotive works at Miles Platting, Manchester and ten by William Fairbairn and Sons, also in Manchester. The first was built in 1849 and most were built by 1854, but a further one was added in 1856, two more in 1869 and one in 1870. All were withdrawn between 1872 and 1886. This particular locomotive has not been identified.

33 L & Y Jenkins express passenger engine

This type of 2-4-0 was the L & Y express passenger engine of the Jenkins era. Twenty-two were built at Miles Platting between 1861 and 1867. The driving wheels were 5ft 9in and the first twelve were initially named after directors of the company. Numbers 15 and 16 were among the last four built, in 1867, and this is a photograph of one of them, probably no 15. Cabs were added in the 1870s and no 15 was withdrawn in 1896, no 16 in 1892. Note the large polished brass dome also visible on no 325.

34 L & Y GNR type 0-4-2

In 1876, by arrangement with the Great Northern Railway, part of an order being built for the GNR by Sharp Stewart and Co was diverted to the L & Y. They were the same as GN 74 class and on that railway they were regarded as mixed traffic engines, but on the L & Y they were used on passenger trains and, until the advent of the 4-4-0s, were in fact the most powerful passenger engines in use. No 647 was Sharp Stewart works number 2582, and was built in May 1876. Driving wheels were 5ft 7½in and trailing wheels 3ft 7½in with 17 × 24in cylinders. The photograph shows the locomotive as it was built, with domeless boiler and GN type cab. They were rebuilt later with domes and with other features altered, no 647 being rebuilt in December 1894. It was withdrawn in 1899.

37 L & Y 4 class

No 51 was one of the later batch of the Yates 4 class 2–4–0s provided with a cab when built in January 1875 at Miles Platting (works number 420). Comparing this with the photograph of nos 4 and 80, some other minor adjustments will be noted, particularly the leading wheel rim splasher round the 3ft 9in diameter leading wheels instead of the fore-and-aft shaped plates on the earlier locomotives. Three of this later batch were also built with domes but most, as no 51, were domeless. No 51 was withdrawn in December 1894.

35 L & Y 4 class

Jenkins' successor, William Yates, built these passenger 2-4-0s with domeless boilers but no cabs. The driving wheels were 6ft, and the cabs were added later in place of the original bent weatherboards. No 4 was built at Miles Platting in October 1870 as works no 316, and was the first of the class. A further eleven were built in 1871 like no 4, but another twelve built in 1872-5 differed from no 4 in having a curved rear splasher and were provided with cabs as new. No 4 carries double headlamps in this photograph.

36 L & Y 4 class

No 80 was also of 4 class, built at Miles Platting works in June 1871 to works number 347. It was rebuilt or reboilered in 1886, but this is not thought to have altered its outward appearance. Seen from the opposite side to no 4, the reversing rod is of course visible. It was withdrawn in August 1898. Notice the old-fashioned hook coupling on the front buffer beam. Although these engines were working express passenger trains it will be seen that no vacuum brakes or vacuum train brake controls had been fitted at this time.

38 L & Y Rebuilt 2-4-0

No 93 was a Yates rebuild of an older Jenkins 2-2-2 built in 1849 and
originally numbered 133, being renumbered 93 in 1850. The rebuild was
carried out in 1872, and in addition to altering it to 2-4-0 a domeless boiler,
a Yates-type cab was fitted. The original outside cylinders were retained, as
can be seen, making it different from the new 2-4-0s. It will also be noted
that the older type of four-wheel tender was also retained, and the open
splashers, giving it an older-looking appearance. It is probable that much of
the older locomotive remained, apart from the boiler and the extra pair of
driving wheels, as it only lasted until 1879 before being withdrawn.

39 L & Y LNW *Newton* **class**
In 1873, the L & Y purchased a
number of Ramsbottom *Newton* type
2-4-0s from the LNW, and no 457
was one of these. It was built at Crewe
works as Crewe number 1673, and
went straight to the L & Y in July
1873. It can be compared with the
photograph of LNW no 1525 as being
the early Webb development of the
Ramsbottom design with the Webb
cab, but still retaining some of the
Ramsbottom features such as the
slotted splashers. In this case, the cab
was provided when it was built. The L
& Y later fitted larger driving wheels
of 6ft 9in instead of 6ft 7½in diameter,
and fitted new boilers slightly smaller
than the original ones. The wrought
iron chimneys were replaced by cast
iron ones, and the splashers were filled
in. No 457 was rebuilt in 1888 and
withdrawn in January 1896.

40 L & Y Shunting tank

These shunting tank engines were basically a continuation of a type designed by Jenkins for shunting on Liverpool dockside lines, but with cabs instead of only weatherboards. Some later had the saddle tanks extended to the front of the smoke box. No 208 was one of thirty-nine built between 1868 and 1875 by Yates, being Miles Platting works number 437 of September 1875. It was withdrawn during the year 1893. The boiler was longer than on the Jenkins locomotives being 10ft 4in long instead of 9ft 6in. The diameter of 3ft 10in was the same.

41 L & Y Barton Wright 0-6-2T

Yates retired in 1875 and William Barton Wright took over as Locomotive Superintendent. His locomotives were well designed and substantially built. This 0-6-2 tank engine design was introduced in 1881 and built by Kitson and Co and Dübs and Co. No 223 was built by the latter company, their works number being 1664 in January 1883, but its original L & Y number was 183, being changed to 223 in 1896. A number of them were reboilered and lasted well into the LMS period, but no 223 was withdrawn in November 1910. The driving wheels were 5ft 1in diameter. It will be noticed that the company crest now also appears on the locomotive in addition to the number and makers' plate.

42 L & Y 978 class

When Barton Wright resigned in 1886 his place was taken by John A.F. Aspinall with the title of Chief Mechanical Engineer. He was later knighted. These were his first express passenger engines, the 978 class built in 1888-9 by Beyer Peacock and Co of Manchester. No 982 was their no 2876, built in August 1888. Driving wheels were 6ft 0in diameter and bogie wheels 3ft 0½in with 18 × 26in cylinders. No 982 was rebuilt in May 1915 with a Belpaire firebox, and in this form it became LMS 10106, surviving until February 1934.

43 L & Y 1093 class

Aspinall's second class of 4-4-0s proved themselves to be very successful, and soon got the nickname of 'Flyers', their large 7ft 3in diameter driving wheels giving them a good turn of speed. They were built at the new locomotive works at Horwich opened in 1888 in place of the former Miles Platting works. His later 4-4-2 design with their high boilers became known as 'High

Flyers'. No 1096, officially of 1093 class, was built in April 1891. Reboilered in 1897 and 1907, it was withdrawn by the LMS in June 1927 but never carried its LMS number, 10153. Some of the class were later fitted with superheaters but not 1096. As will be seen the tender was lettered 'Lancashire & Yorkshire' in addition to the crest on the leading splasher.

45 L & Y 1220 class

No 1228 (also of 1220 class) seen here on shed, and the company crest is very clearly shown. It was built in the same month as 1226 and was reboilered in July 1918. Only one locomotive of the class was ever superheated (no 455), and this and two others were given Belpaire boilers although 1228, like 1226, always had a round top boiler. It did not survive long enough to be given its LMS number 10173, being withdrawn in May 1927. The water columns with gas lamps on top are of interest.

44 L & Y 1220 class

This locomotive belonged to Aspinall's third class of 4-4-0s. They were similar to the 1093 class, with 7ft 3in diameter driving wheels but the cylinders were slightly smaller, being 18 × 26in compared to 19 × 26in on the 1093 class. It was officially known as 1220 class and they were also built at Horwich. No 1226 was built in February 1894, and was reboilered in July 1917. It lasted a little longer than 1096, until September 1928, and did receive its LMS number 10171. This photograph is of earlier date than that of 1096, before lettering on the tender was introduced in 1904.

46 L & Y Hughes 2-6-2T

Aspinall was appointed General Manager of the L & Y in 1899 and his place as Chief Mechanical Engineer was taken by the former Horwich works manager, Henry Albert Hoy. He resigned after only five years in 1904, and this class of locomotive was the only one he designed for the L & Y, very different from the others. It was intended for use on heavy local passenger work on the many steeply-graded lines and had 2,000 gallons water capacity and vacuum-operated water scoops. When they were built, they were the largest tank engines in the UK. Superheated 2-4-2 tank engines replaced them on passenger trains after 1914, when they were transferred to shunting work. No 1441 was built at Horwich in April 1904, reboilered in June 1914 and withdrawn in August 1926, and did not carry its LMS number 11707. Twenty were built between 1903 and 1904.

47 L & Y ex-East Lancashire Railway

The L & Y amalgamated with the East Lancashire Railway in 1859, but
until 1875 they operated it as a separate division centred on the East
Lancashire works at Bury. The ELR locomotives all carried names, and for a
time they were retained after the locomotives were amalgamated into one
number sequence in 1875 by adding 600 to the ELR numbers. No 629 was
built as ELR no 29 *Ariel* in October 1848, by Walker Bros of Bury, and
rebuilt in October 1868. It is seen here after the fitting of an LNW-type cab
in the 1870s. It was replaced by a new locomotive in August 1886.

48 L & Y ex-East Lancashire Railway

No 656 was also built by Walker Bros of Bury as ELR no 56 *Agamemnon* in
January 1853, and was rebuilt with a new long boiler with polished brass
dome cover in January 1868. Driving wheels were 4ft 9in diameter and the
cylinders were increased from 15 × 24in to 16 × 24in. This type of
locomotive was known generally as 'long boiler type', a design originally
produced by the firm of Robert Stephenson and Co. The little girl was
possibly the driver's daughter, and the photograph was probably taken on a
Sunday morning when driver and locomotive would not be working.
Agamemnon was replaced in July 1881.

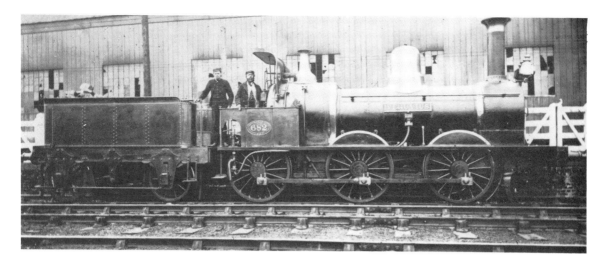

49 L & Y (East Lancashire Division) 303 class

No 682 was built after the amalgamation as EL Division 82 *Vesuvius* in
September 1864, and was of Jenkins design as L & Y 303 class standard
goods engine. It was built at Miles Platting (works no 187). This photograph
shows the original form of this class before cabs were added in the 1870s.
Most of the class were rebuilt as 0–6–0 saddle tank engines with 4ft 0in
diameter wheels instead of 4ft 10in in the 1880s. No 682, however, was
altered in July 1882 to an 0–6–2 tank engine with the 4ft 10in diameter
wheels retained and cylinders increased from 16in to 17in diameter. By then
the name had been removed. It was withdrawn in 1898.

50 L & Y (East Lancashire Division) 303 class Rebuilt

When first built at Miles Platting in May 1867 as EL Division 90 with the
name *Sisyphus* (works no 247), no 690 looked like no 682 and 693 as it was of
the same class. This photograph shows the locomotive after rebuilding in
October 1884 as an 0–6–0 saddle tank engine with 4ft 0in diameter wheels
instead of 4ft 10in. As will be seen, the rebuilding was very extensive and a
very much more modern-looking locomotive was produced. No 690 was
withdrawn in 1898. In this photograph it carries a re-railing jack on the front
buffer beam for dealing with minor derailments in goods yards, where track
was not maintained to a very high standard.

53 L & Y (East Lancashire Division) Shunting tank
This was of the same class as L & Y no 208, six being built additionally for the EL Division at Miles Platting in 1875. No 620 *Vulcan* was works number 326 in April of that year. Comparing this photograph with that of no 208 (plate 40) built five months later, it will be seen that no 620's cab was rather less substantial: it had no side sheets and was possibly originally provided only with a weatherboard. The man in the middle appears to be holding forth quite forcibly about something. Perhaps it was a good story! No 620 was withdrawn in 1897.

51 L & Y (East Lancashire Division) 303 class

Another photograph of the Jenkins 303 class 0–6–0 built for the EL Division at Miles Platting. No 693 was originally EL Division 93 *Tantalus,* and was Miles Platting works no 255 of November 1867. Like no 690, no 693 was rebuilt as an 0–6–0 saddle tank engine, 693 being so altered in May 1885. As on the photograph of 682, it will be noted that the re-railing jack was carried on the footplate and the side plate was cut away to facilitate its removal.

52 L & Y (East Lancashire Division) 32 class

These 2–4–0 saddle tank engines were designed by William Yates to work passenger trains over any part of the system except the Werneth incline in Oldham. They were known as 32 class. Twenty were built between 1868 and 1874 for the main division of the L & Y, and five in 1870 and 1873 for the East Lancashire Division. No 623 was originally EL Division no 23 *Elk,* built in July 1870 as Miles Platting works no 308. They were originally well tank engines, the saddle tanks being added later to improve water capacity. They proved to be underpowered and they had a short life, most being withdrawn in the 1880s. No 623, which was rebuilt in November 1877 was not, however, withdrawn until 1893. As will be seen, the nameplate on *Elk* was fitted to the splasher rather than the more usual place on the tank side.

55 Unidentified 2-2-0

This engine is probably of early L & Y origin, but this cannot be verified with any certainty. As shown here it is not in its original form, having been converted from a tender engine to a tank engine by the rather clumsy addition of a saddle tank of square section. The smokebox and chimney may also have been replaced. The 'haystack' firebox suggests that the locomotive was of Bury type, some of which were supplied to the Manchester and Bolton and other railways absorbed by the L & Y. Many were sold to private industrial firms by the L & Y as they quickly became unsuitable for main line use due to their small size, and this locomotive is thought to have been one of them.

54 L & Y (ex-Manchester and Leeds) 54 class

This Bury 0-4-0 was one of fifteen ordered from the firm of Bury, Curtis and Kennedy by the Manchester and Leeds Railway in 1845; delivery commenced in March 1847. In the same month, the M & L changed its name to Lancashire and Yorkshire. The M & L had already amalgamated with the Manchester and Bolton Railway in 1846, and some of the locomotives went to this section as well as to the M & L line. The identity of this locomotive is not known, but the last one was not withdrawn until 1880. This, however, was one of ten rebuilt in the 1860s as 0-4-2. The last unrebuilt one was L & Y no 193 withdrawn for scrapping in 1875. The chimney and smokebox on the locomotive are later replacements probably dating from about 1862, but the typical 'haystack' firebox provided on Bury locomotives is still retained.

6
Companies associated with the West Coast and Midland Routes

Furness Railway

Connected to both the Midland Railway and the L & NW at Carnforth and running through Barrow-in-Furness to Whitehaven, iron ore and mineral traffic for the local iron and steel and shipbuilding industries was the chief source of revenue. Barrow was virtually created by the railway but attempts to turn it into a major port were not successful.

The Sharp 0-6-0 seen in plate 56 was built for the mineral traffic. During this period the company relied on manufacturer's designs for its locomotives. Charles Patrick Stewart joined the firm of Sharp Brothers and Company in 1852 when John and Thomas Sharp retired. They had built their first locomotive for the Liverpool and Manchester railway in 1833. The firm became Sharp Stewart and Company and was at Great Bridgewater Street in Manchester, but moved to Glasgow in 1888 and became part of the North British Locomotive Company in 1903. Stewart was influential in introducing the Giffard patent injector to this country on which the firm held sole rights.

Caledonian Railway

The Caledonian was the largest railway in Scotland, and although it routed its English traffic via the L & NW West Coast route, it also reached the East Coast at Edinburgh and Aberdeen via Forfar, although this route has now been closed.

The firm of Neilson and Company was founded by Walter Montgomerie Neilson in 1836 and built its first locomotive in 1843 for the Glasgow, Garnkirk and Coatbridge Railway, a constituent of the Caledonian Railway. It amalgamated with Sharp Stewart and Company and Dübs and Company in 1903 to form the North British Locomotive Company. Neilson's Hyde Park works, opened in 1861, was adjacent to those of the Caledonian and North British railways in Springburn, Glasgow. They were prolific builders for railways all over the world, but particularly popular with Scottish railways including the tiny Solway Junction Railway (plate 57).

Dugald Drummond, a man of strong personality who could be obstinate and agressive, came to the Caledonian Railway from the North British Railway where he had achieved some success in modernising their locomotives. He established a similar tradition on the Caledonian with the 80 class 4-4-0s (plate 58) which was continued by his successors when he left in 1890. In 1895 the London and South Western railway locomotive department was placed in his charge.

Glasgow and South Western Railway

This railway had its works at Kilmarnock and operated to the Ayrshire coast, Dumfries, Stranraer and to Gretna from where it reached Carlisle via the Caledonian line. Its English operating partner was the Midland Railway and its Glasgow terminus the former St Enoch station. Before 1923 no less than seven companies operated into Carlisle.

James Stirling succeeded his brother Patrick who left to go to the Great Northern Railway in 1866. He introduced many improvements including his own design of bogie and a steam reversing gear. In 1874 he was the first to provide cushioned seats in third class carriages.

The 0-4-2 mixed traffic engines (plate 59) were popular on the G & SW and ninety were built by him between 1870 and 1878 when he was appointed locomotive superintendent of the South Eastern railway.

Hugh Smellie succeeded James Stirling at Kilmarnock. His designs were noted for their free steaming qualities and simplicity of layout, resulting in low maintenance costs with graceful lines generally following the Stirling tradition. The 153 class were particularly successful (plate 60) and worked the through St Pancras to Glasgow Pullman trains in conjunction with the Midland Railway. Under his direction, steam brakes were introduced on goods engines and vacuum brakes on passenger trains. In 1890 he became locomotive superintendent on the Caledonian Railway.

Highland Railway

The most northerly railway in the British Isles, the Highland connected with the Caledonian at Perth and its works were at Inverness.

One of its most prominent engineers was David Jones who came from Manchester and was an apprentice under Ramsbottom. He was in charge at Inverness for twenty-seven years from 1860. As well as rebuilding the older locomotives (plate 61) he introduced several famous classes of 4-4-0 and the 'large goods' in 1894, the first British 4-6-0.

Peter Drummond, the younger brother of Dugald, took over from Jones in 1896 and introduced the *Ben* 4-4-0s (plate 62) and the *Castle* 4-6-0s, a development of the Jones 'large goods' for passenger traffic.

North Staffordshire Railway

Centred on Stoke-on-Trent the North Staffordshire Railway later built many of its own locomotives there, but the original engines came from outside suppliers. John Curphey Forsyth who ordered the single in plate 63 from Kitson and Company was the first resident engineer on the line.

Kitson and Company were founded in Leeds as Todd, Kitson and Laird in 1836. Partners changed frequently in the period up to 1863 when the above title was adopted.

East and West Junction Railway

This railway connected with the L & NW at Roade and also had connections with the Midland and Great Western Railways. It was a cross-country line through Stratford-upon-Avon, and had a somewhat precarious financial existence.

The famous firm of Beyer Peacock and Company who built the locomotive in plate 64 was founded at Gorton in Manchester in 1854 by Charles Frederick Beyer, who had been a designer for Sharp Brothers and Company (later Sharp Stewart) and Richard Peacock, who was locomotive superintendent for the Manchester, Sheffield and Lincolnshire Railway.

Belfast and Northern Counties Railway

The Midland Railway route to Ireland was via Heysham and its eventual takeover of this railway was a natural extension. The Irish standard gauge of 5ft 3in was imposed by Parliament in 1843 as a compromise three years before the Gauge Act of 1846.

B & NC livery was a rather dull 'invisible green'. Compare the Sharp 0-6-0 (plate 65) with the Furness locomotive (plate 56) also built by Sharp Stewart.

All the above companies, along with the L & NW, Midland, L & Y and some smaller ones, were formed into the London Midland and Scottish railway in 1923.

56 Furness 29 class

This was one of many locomotives on the Furness designed for them by Sharp
Stewart and Co and known affectionately as 'Sharpies'. No 76 was built in
1873, being SS works no 2280. The driving wheels were 4ft 6½in diameter
and the four-wheel tender carried 1,500 gallons of water. They were later
provided with larger six-wheel tenders. These small engines, with 16 × 24in
cylinders, proved to be hard-working and efficient and many, including no
76, passed into LMS ownership. No 76 became LMS 12006 and was
withdrawn in 1925, being scrapped in December 1926.

57 Caledonian (ex-Solway Junction)

This locomotive was ordered by the Solway Junction Railway, which was
opened from Kirtlebridge to Brayton via a viaduct crossing the Solway Firth
in 1869. By the time of opening, the company had agreed a working
arrangement with the Caledonian Railway whose line made a connection
with the railway at Kirtlebridge. The seven locomotives it had purchased
passed into CR stock. This 0–4–2 well tank engine was built by Neilson and
Co, works number 1217 in 1866 and became CR no 541. In 1892 it was
transferred to duplicate stock as 541A, as seen here. It was again renumbered
in 1899, which dates the photograph to the 1892–9 period. It was withdrawn
in 1900. The canopy was added later, and the locomotive was originally
intended for the Northampton and Banbury Junction Railway.

58 Caledonian 80 class

Dugald Drummond designed this locomotive for the CR before he left their employ in 1890 to start his own business. It was not built until 1891 at the CR locomotive works at St Rollox in Glasgow, to order Y28. Certain modifications, including a slightly larger boiler, were made to the Drummond design by his successor, Hugh Smellie. Officially regarded as 80 class, they were often referred to as 'Coast Bogies' since they were put to working the Glasgow to Gourock line. Driving wheels were 5ft 9in diameter and they had 18 × 26in cylinders. No 195 went to the duplicate list as 1195 in 1922 and was withdrawn in 1923. Drummond, of course, later joined the London and South Western Railway.

59 Glasgow and South Western 221 class

James Stirling was the younger brother of Patrick Stirling, under whom he was apprenticed on the Great Northern Railway. He was strongly influenced by his brother's designs, including the use of the domeless boiler, when he designed this 0–4–2 mixed traffic locomotive of 221 class for the G & SW. Fifty were built between 1874 and 1878. The Ramsbottom safety valves without cover were originally fitted above the firebox, but the later locomotives had them fitted in the position seen here. No 275 was built by Neilson and Co to order 481, works no 2341, in May 1878. It became duplicate list no 275A in January 1909, and no 649 in 1919, eventually becoming LMS 17045; it was withdrawn in January 1925.

61 Highland (ex-Inverness and Aberdeen Junction)

The Inverness and Aberdeen Junction Railway changed its name to Highland in 1865, the year after this locomotive was built (April 1864) by Sharp Stewart and Co, works number 1508. It was originally named *Kincraig*. The photograph shows the locomotive after rebuilding by David Jones with a new boiler, the original boilers being domeless, and a cab, or to use Jones's term 'house'. This rebuilding was carried out in September 1891, and the locomotive was withdrawn in August 1902. As will be seen by comparing this photograph with LNW 137, 349 and 161 (plates 14-16), this locomotive was an enlarged version of the 'Crewe' type.

60 Glasgow and South Western 153 class

Built for main line express work by Hugh Smellie, Stirling's successor before he himself went to the Caledonian Railway, some of Stirling's influence can still be seen in this 153 class of 1886–9, including the cab and domeless boiler. All twenty were built at the G & SW works at Kilmarnock, no 66 being works no 205 of June 1887. By this date automatic vacuum brakes were fitted to all passenger trains, although some companies used the air-brake Westinghouse system instead. The engine number is repeated on the tender inside a scroll. No 66 became 454 in 1919, and was reboilered in 1923 when it became LMS 14147. The LMS fitted it with Westinghouse brakes for working with Caledonian stock. It was withdrawn in November 1932.

62 Highland 'Large Ben' (U class)

These locmotives were known as large (or new) 'Ben' class since they were all named after Scottish Bens, but the official classification was simply U. The locomotive seen here as LMS 14418, was originally HR no 63. It was designed by Peter Drummond, the younger brother of Dugald, and was one of the first four built in 1908 with six-wheel tenders. No 63, which was North British Locomotive Co works number 17399 of May 1908, was coupled to a double-bogie tender soon afterwards. The other five also received them, the last two of the six locomotives built being so fitted when built. No 63 was fitted for both vacuum and Westinghouse brake working and was withdrawn in December 1932. There were also twenty small Bens with smaller boilers.

65 Belfast and Northern Counties

Built in July 1861 by Sharp Stewart and Co, works number 1277, for the 5ft 3in gauge B & NC, this photograph shows the locomotive in its original condition with 4ft 6in diameter wheels and 16 × 24in cylinders, and with only a weatherboard. It was rebuilt with 17in diameter cylinders in 1883, by which time a cab had probably been added, and again rebuilt in 1902. The B & NC was acquired by the Midland Railway in 1903 and administered by a Northern Counties Committee. It is now Northern Ireland Railways. No 35 was withdrawn in November 1925.

63 North Staffordshire 54 class

This was one of the locomotives ordered for the NSR by the original engineers, S.P. Bidder and J.C. Forsyth, and was built by the firm of Kitson Thompson and Hewitson, works number 241 in 1851. The photograph shows no 57 as built with weatherboard only, before it was equipped with a shallow round cab. It was renumbered 25 in 1870 and replaced by a 2–4–0 tank in 1882. The Salter safety valve is fixed to the dome, and it has what was known as a bell-capped chimney. The first sections of the NSR were opened in 1848–9 and the railway was centred on Stoke-on-Trent.

64 East and West Junction

Beyer Peacock and Co built this saddle tank engine for the East and West Junction Railway which eventually became the Stratford-upon-Avon and Midland Junction Railway. It was BP order 3721, works no 1830 and was built in August 1879. It was sold by the E & WJ in April 1890 to Rothervale Colliery as their no 1, and the photograph shows the locomotive after the sale with Rothervale number plate. Like many locomotives sold by the main line railways to collieries it had a long life, surviving to become National Coal Board property. It was not scrapped until October 1959, although from 1929 it carried the unusual number 0.

7
East Coast Companies and the Great Central

Stockton and Darlington Railway

This pioneer railway, which was the first public railway to use locomotives in 1825 when it opened (although horse haulage was also used) had developed considerably by the time its locomotive engineer William Bouch, successor to Timothy Hackworth, designed the 4-4-0 in plate 66. It had just extended westward over the wilds of Stainmore to connect with the L & NW and the Midland Railway main lines. The S & D amalgamated with the North Eastern Railway in 1863 but continued as a separate division for ten years.

North Eastern Railway

Along with the Great Northern Railway to the south and the North British Railway in Scotland, the NE formed the central part of the East Coast route and, in fact, operated express trains over the North British line to Edinburgh, taking over from the Great Northern Railway at York. It also had a line to Carlisle from Newcastle-on-Tyne and extensive lines in North East England. Heavy mineral traffic was an important feature.

Edward Fletcher was their first locomotive engineer from 1854 to 1882. Apprenticed to the Stephenson's, he was popular with his men and allowed district engineers considerable scope in design features at the four works then functioning at Gateshead, Leeds, York and, from 1863, Darlington, making no attempt at a standardised policy.

The 708 class (plate 67) were in fact the earliest to be constructed as a class with any unity of design and were built by outside manufacturers.

By the time Wilson Worsdell took over from his elder brother T.W. Worsdell in 1890 the locomotive policy was altogether different, with standard classes being built as on other railways. His brother had built a large number of compound 0-6-0s as well as compound passenger classes. These were to the Worsdell von Bories system which had two cylinders, one high-pressure and one low-pressure, both inside the frames with a patent starting valve. There were thus only two exhausts per revolution, resulting in a very slow-sounding beat.

Wilson Worsdell did not, however, share his brother's enthusiasm for compounding and designed simple expansion engines, ultimately rebuilding the compounds. The P class 0-6-0s (plate 68) were the first of four classes built under his direction.

Great Central Railway

Originally known as the Manchester, Sheffield and Lincolnshire Railway, the GC opened its extension to London, Marylebone in 1899. John George Robinson had been in charge of the locomotives of the Waterford,

Limerick and Western railway in Ireland before coming to the GC in 1902, and his designs were noted for their handsome lines. He devoted himself to the development of superheating and in 1911 he perfected the superheater that bore his name, which was ultimately widely used along with the Schmidt type. Amongst other inventions he designed a force-feed lubricator and anti-collision buffers on coaches.

The 4–4–0s of his design (plate 69) and *Atlantics* (plate 70) were amongst his most celebrated classes. When the LNER was formed in 1923 he was offered the post of chief mechanical engineer but decided to retire.

North British Railway

The North British Railway, which joined the NE at Berwick-on-Tweed, was the Scottish link in the East Coast route, providing onward connection to Glasgow, Queen Street and Aberdeen via Dundee. In addition it had a line, now closed, from Edinburgh to Carlisle via Galashiels often known as the 'Waverley Route' over which it operated the Edinburgh traffic of the Midland Railway.

William Hurst came to the NB in 1855 and fourteen of the 0–4–2 well tank engines (plate 71) were built between 1857 and 1864. Unfortunately his employment with the NB terminated under a cloud when he was dismissed in 1866 as a result of some financial dealings to his own advantage but at the expense of the company.

Thomas Wheatley was appointed in 1867 to succeed Hurst. The 2–4–0 of 48 class (plate 72) was the last of this wheel arrangement on the NB, eight being built between 1866–8. In 1871 Wheatley brought out his 4–4–0 224 class which were the first inside cylinder 4–4–0s in Britain. Number 224 itself was the locomotive that went down with the first Tay bridge in 1879, but it was later recovered and repaired.

Like Hurst before him Wheatley was also dismissed for dishonest dealings in 1874 and set up as a private contractor the following year. He was succeeded by Dugald Drummond until 1882 when Matthew Holmes was appointed as locomotive engineer. He had been Drummond's assistant, the NB owning at this time 835 engines. He introduced several classes of 4–4–0, the 633 class (plate 73) being built in 1890–5. He was, in contrast to his predecessor, a likeable man much respected by all.

The East Coast companies along with the Great Eastern, Great Central and Great North of Scotland railways, became the London and North Eastern Railway in 1923.

Eastern and Midlands Railway (later Midland and Great Northern Joint)

The locomotive engineer of this railway was William Marriott, from its inception with the amalgamation of two local lines in Norfolk in 1883 until he retired in 1924. However the 4–4–0 in plate 74 was of Beyer Peacock design. The E & M had thirty-five locomotives when the Joint Board was formed in 1894 and eighty-six when the locomotives became LNER property in 1936.

67 North Eastern 708 class

During Edward Fletcher's period of office as Locomotive Superintendent of the NER there was little attempt at standardisation. The 708 class illustrated here was the first large group of locomotives ordered by Fletcher that could be regarded as a class, although some degree of standardisation was applied to many of the others later on. Later locomotives had inside cylinders instead of the outside ones used on this class. No 774 was built by R & W Hawthorn and Co, works number 1539 in April 1873 at their Forth Bank works in Newcastle. It was replaced in NE locomotive stock in 1911. Note the rather unusual lamp position at the side of the smokebox. Driving wheels were 5ft 0in diameter and cylinders 17 × 24in.

66 Stockton and Darlington

This was one of four 4-4-0s built in 1862 by R. Stephenson and Co, works number 1335. No 165 *Keswick* had 7ft 0½in diameter driving wheels and 16 × 24in cylinders. Thomas Bouch, the Stockton and Darlington Locomotive Superintendent, designed these locomotives for working over the newly-opened Stainmore summit line of the S & D, although what the driving conditions must have been like with only a weatherboard for protection defies imagination. The large driving wheels and outside frames certainly gave them an impressive appearance. The S & D locomotives passed into North Eastern locomotive stock in 1874, and 1000 was added to the numbers so that no 165 became NE 1165. It was scrapped in 1886.

68 North Eastern P class

This photograph well illustrates the development of the 0-6-0 during the twenty-five years from 1873, when 774 was built, to 1898 when 1952 was built at the NE works at Darlington to the designs of Wilson Worsdell. One of the last of seventy locomotives of P class with 4ft 7¼in diameter wheels and 18 × 24in cylinders, no 1952 was turned out in June 1898. Subsequent developments were the P1, P2 and P3 classes. NE locomotives retained their original numbers when they passed to the LNER in 1923, and this one was withdrawn in August 1933 without any significant rebuilding as LNE class J24.

69 Great Central 11B class

John George Robinson was appointed Chief Mechanical Engineer of the GC in 1902, and this 11B class was the first of several classes of 4-4-0 designed by him. The company had already opened its London extension into Marylebone, changing its name from the Manchester, Sheffield and Lincolnshire Railway to Great Central Railway, and these locomotives were designed to work the London expresses. The 11B class had 6ft 8in diameter driving wheels and $18\frac{1}{2} \times 26$in cylinders. No 1038 was built by Sharp Stewart and Co, works number 4964, in March 1903. In October 1914 the cylinders were increased to 20in diameter and it was superheated, becoming 11D class. It became LNER 6038, and was renumbered 2322 in 1946. On the LNER its classification was D9.

70 Great Central 8D class

This was Robinson's Atlantic design for the GC, which were built from 1903
as GC class 8B. No 258 was a compound version of these as GC class 8D.
They were nicknamed 'Jersey Lilies' in the Manchester area but this was not,
as was thought in the south, an allusion to the actress Lily Langtry, but to a
Manchester pub act featuring a fat lady, and was on account of their size
rather than their graceful lines and proportions. No 258 was built at the GC
works at Gorton, Manchester in December 1905. Named in 1909 *The Right
Hon Vincent Cross GCB GCSI*, it had 6ft 9in diameter driving wheels, an inside
high-pressure cylinder of 19 × 26in and two outside low-pressure cylinders of
21 × 26in. Withdrawn as LNER C5 class 2895 at the end of 1946, it was
superheated from 1927.

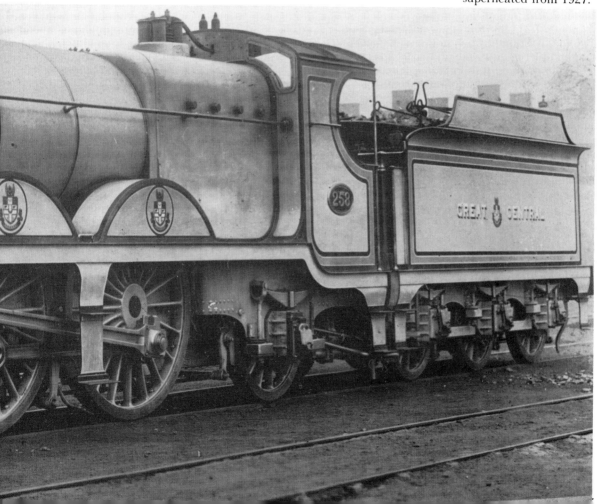

73 North British 633 class

These rather handsome 4-4-0s were designed by Matthew Holmes, who was Locomotive Superintendent of the NBR from 1882 until 1903. In general he followed the trend set by his predecessor, Dugald Drummond, but his adoption of the Great Northern type of round half-cab was probably rather a retrograde step in the 1890s when these 4-4-0s were built. No 211 was of 633 class built at Cowlairs in January 1895, with 6ft 6in diameter driving wheels and 18 × 26in cylinders. This photograph, possibly an official one, shows the locomotive as it was built, but it was rebuilt in September 1922 and withdrawn as LNER class D31 in September 1937.

71 North British 20 class

The North British Railway established their works at St Margaret's, Meadowbank, Edinburgh in 1844, but locomotive building there did not commence until 1856. This rather ungainly 0-4-2 well tank engine was the third locomotive built there in 1857, with 4ft 9in diameter driving wheels and 12 × 18in cylinders. It was hired to the contractors building the Girvan and Portpatrick Junction Railway which opened in 1876, and was purchased by T. Wheatley who had a contract to provide locomotives for the Wigtownshire Railway. It was later named *Lochinvar* and rebuilt as an 0-4-2 saddle tank engine.

72 North British 418 class

After amalgamation with the Edinburgh and Glasgow Railway in 1865, locomotive building was transferred to the E & G works in Glasgow at Cowlairs, which is where this 2-4-0 was built in 1873 with 6ft 0in diameter driving wheels and 16 × 22in cylinders. Originally no 428 *Ratho*, the number changed to 1249 in 1914 when it went to the duplicate list. After originally being given the LNE number 9990 it was numbered 10249 in 1925. It was originally to the design of Thomas Wheatley, who was then in charge of the locomotive affairs at Cowlairs before setting up as a private contractor in Wigtownshire. In January 1891 it was rebuilt with 6ft 1in diameter driving wheels and 17 × 24in cylinders and was withdrawn by the LNER in August 1926.

74 Eastern and Midlands

The Eastern and Midlands Railway took over the locomotive stock of the Yarmouth and North Norfolk Railway and the Lynn and Fakenham Railway in 1882. It was transferred to the Midland and Great Northern Joint Committee in 1893, remaining a separate entity until nationalisation in 1948. This outside cylinder 4-4-0 was built by Beyer Peacock and Co to their number 2794 in 1886. The driving wheels were 6ft 0in diameter and the cylinder size was 17 × 24in. No 29 retained its number on the M & GN Joint, being rebuilt in 1906 and scrapped in 1933. It will be seen that the locomotive only just fits the turntable.

8
Great Western Railway

I.K. Brunel, as is well known, built the original line of the GW from Paddington to Bristol to the broad gauge, and it was opened in stages between 1838 and 1841. Brunel himself supplied the specifications for the first locomotives, but although a brilliant civil engineer, he had no experience in mechanical engineering and they were failures.

It fell to the then only twenty-one year old Sir Daniel Gooch, to bring order out of chaos, often labouring through the night to keep the locomotives running. After some brushes with his redoubtable chief, very much his senior in years and reputation, he was eventually given a free hand and ordered reliable engines from Robert Stephenson and Co for whom he had worked for nearly a year in 1835-6.

The broad gauge engines were not a separate type but standard Stephenson types extended to suit the wider gauge. One of these, *North Star*, a 2-2-2, was preserved at Swindon but regrettably broken up in 1906. However a replica was built in 1925 by apprentices and this is now in the Swindon Railway Museum.

The first locomotives of Gooch's own design appeared in 1840 (*Firefly* class) and it was Gooch's decision to site the GW works at Swindon at the junction of the Bristol and Gloucester (later South Wales) lines. The first engine built there was the 2-2-2 *Great Western* in 1846. Gooch produced the stationary link motion, a variation of Stephenson link motion in which the die block was moved up and down instead of the curved link. The *Victoria* 2-4-0s were built in 1856-64, there being eighteen in number (plates 75, 76).

Joseph Armstrong followed Gooch in 1864. He had been in charge of the Wolverhampton works of the Shrewsbury and Birmingham Railway, which also served the Shrewsbury and Chester Railway and which, when merged with the GW in 1854, formed a standard gauge Northern Division. The broad gauge had reached Wolverhampton, with mixed gauge between there and Birmingham (Snow Hill).

By this time the Gauge Act had put an end to any further extension of the broad gauge system which now ran to Milford Haven, Hereford and Penzance as well as Wolverhampton. Consequently Armstrong built few new broad gauge engines but the *Iron Duke* class were renewed (plate 77) and absorption of other broad gauge railways brought more broad gauge engines into GW stock, although these companies also possessed standard gauge locomotives as well. The South Devon tank engine (plate 78), intended to be broad gauge, was completed as a standard gauge locomotive.

In his thirteen years at Swindon 600 new engines were built. His first singles were the 378 class (1865-9, plate 79) and he built seventy-one 2-4-0s (plate 81) eighteen of which were built at Wolverhampton where large numbers of tank engines were also built. He also introduced the standard 0-6-0 with double frames in 1866.

William Dean also progressed to Swindon from Wolverhampton, having been Armstrong's assistant since 1868; he equipped the GW with a stable of strong, simple and efficient engines. He renewed Gooch's 157 class singles (plate 80) and added a further thirty 2-2-2s in 1891–2 (later converted to 3031 class 4-2-2s as seen in plates 88 and 89). He also continued the construction of standard goods, updating the design in 1893, and introduced the 4-4-0 type in the *Badminton* and *Bulldog* classes. He added a further eighty 'Metro' tank engines (plate 82) to the sixty already built by Armstrong and built some experimental types (plate 83) including a 4-2-4 tank with 7ft 8in driving wheels, which was not, however, a success.

Armstrong had already provided over 300 six-coupled saddle tank engines for goods and shunting duties, and Dean more than doubled this number; it became a ubiquitous type on the GW for the rest of its existence (plates 84-7).

By the end of the century, further absorptions had extended the system considerably. Mixed gauge already extended to 455 miles out of the 668 miles of broad gauge lines when the broad gauge was finally abandoned on Friday 29 May 1892. Some engines and many coaches had been built 'convertible' to the standard gauge for some years anticipating the final conversion.

George Jackson Churchward; a quiet unobtrusive man of some considerable ability, had been Dean's assistant since 1897, and as Dean had suffered failing health in his later years, Churchward had increasingly taken over responsibility from him. He experimented with new boiler designs, on which he was to have a worldwide influence, and the Belpaire firebox such as on the *City* class (plate 91) but first fitted on the *Badminton* class (plate 90) built in 1897–8. He was responsible for the introduction of the coned boiler which became a prominent feature of later GW practice as on later batches of the *Bulldog* class (plates 92, 93) and *Saint* class 4-6-0s (plates 95, 96) based on the prototype 4-6-0 (plate 94).

Churchward also experimented with the French de Glehn system of four-cylinder compounding, three compound *Atlantics* being built in France and an experimental *Atlantic* with four high-pressure cylinders at Swindon. These, however, were not perpetuated and 4-6-0s were adopted for main line passenger work with simple expansion.

In February 1908 a *Pacific* locomotive, *The Great Bear*, was built, but it suffered from serious weight restrictions, being the largest in the country at the time; it could only be used between London and Bristol.

Churchward also designed a 'Swindon' pattern superheater, and an improved design of deep narrow piston ring reducing steam leakage. He also introduced 2-8-0 goods engines and later the first 2-8-0 tank engines in Britain. The tank engines for passenger trains which appeared from 1900 were 2-4-2 tanks of 3600 class (plate 97), supplementing Dean's 0-4-2 tank engines on branch lines and 4-4-2 *County* (or *Country*) tank engines (plate 98) and 2-6-2 tank engines (plates 99, 100) for secondary services.

75 Great Western (Broad Gauge) *Victoria* **class**

The original gauge of the Great Western and some of the railways associated
with it was 7ft 0½in, as recommended by the company's engineer, I.K.
Brunel. The now famous works at Swindon were completed by 1843–5 and
Daniel Gooch, the Locomotive Superintendent, produced the first locomotives
to be built there in 1846. The broad gauge engines were not numbered, only
named, and *Fulton* was of *Victoria* class built to the sixth passenger lot in
January 1864. The wheels were 6ft 6in diameter and the cylinders were 16 ×
24in. Note the seat for the guard on the tender in this original photograph.
Fulton was withdrawn from traffic in November 1876.

76 Great Western (Broad Gauge) *Victoria* **class**
Telford was also of *Victoria* class built to the same lot in April 1864. As on
Fulton, although not very clear in that photograph, the handrails extended
round the front of the smokebox. The locomotive had compensating levers
between all axles and the domeless boilers had the regulator box on the front
tube plate. *Telford* had a slightly longer life than *Fulton*, being withdrawn in
February 1879.

77 Great Western (Broad Gauge) *Iron Duke* **class**
Daniel Gooch left the GW in 1864 to join the Telegraph Construction
Company, which chartered Brunel's ship *Great Eastern* to lay the first
transatlantic cable. He was eventually made a baronet. He returned to the
GW as Chairman in 1865. His place was taken by Joseph Armstrong, who
had formerly been in charge of the narrow gauge works at Wolverhampton
but now became Locomotive Superintendent of the whole railway. Only
forty-two more broad gauge locomotives were built at Swindon, including
renewals of the *Iron Duke* class of 1847–50 of which *Sultan* was one. The last
fifteen of these were produced by William Dean, who succeeded Armstrong in
1877. Some further locmotives were built which were convertible from broad
gauge to standard gauge. The renewed 4-2-2s were provided with half-cabs.
Sultan was built in September 1876 and scrapped in May 1892, when the
broad gauge was abandoned.

78 Great Western (ex-South Devon)

This tank engine was erected at Swindon from parts supplied by the Ince Forge Co, Wigan to the South Devon Railway. They were intended for the broad gauge but were still incomplete when the SD amalgamated with the GW in 1876. It was turned out, with two others from the same source, as a narrow (or standard) gauge engine in November 1878 and fitted with a crane in 1881. The South Devon Railway had intended to name this locomotive *Jupiter*. No 1299 became service stock in May 1829 and was withdrawn in Septmber 1936.

79 Great Western (Standard Gauge) 378 class

This locomotive was built at Swindon to lot no 19, works no 185. It was one of Armstrong's first passenger class, the 378 or *Sir Daniel* class, of which thirty were built in 1866 and 1869, no 584 being built in July 1869. Its original number was 1119, but this was changed to 584 in 1870. In 1900-02 they had become redundant on main line passenger trains because they were too small. Rather unusually, nearly all of them, including 584, were rebuilt as 0-6-0 goods engines with 5ft 2in diameter driving wheels in place of the original single pair of 7ft 0in diameter driving wheels. Cabs were fitted to them as singles at a later date. No 584 was withdrawn in October 1911.

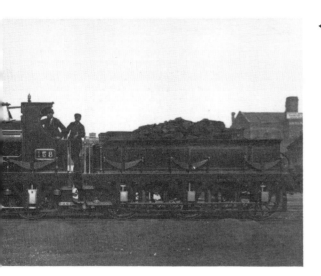

80 GW 157 class

These were renewals of earlier locomotives built in 1862, and were known as 157 or *Cobham* class. No 158 was built at Swindon to lot 51, works number 815 and was originally named *Worcester* until the name was removed in 1895. The building date was September 1879 and no 158 was reboiled in 1886 and 1890, but not otherwise rebuilt. The locomotive appears here in extremely smart condition, the polish on the brass work literally glinting in the sunlight. Driving wheels were 7ft 0in diameter as on the 378 class, and the cylinders were 18 × 24in. Number 158 was withdrawn in June 1905.

81 GW 6ft 2-4-0

No 726 was one of eleven built by Armstrong in 1871–2 with 6ft 0in diameter driving wheels and 17 × 24in cylinders. It was built to Swindon lot 29, works number 401 in September 1872, and reboiled with a Wolverhampton boiler in 1887 and a Swindon type in 1898, 1903 and 1912. Cabs were added to the class in the late 1870s. Again the brasswork gleams, including the dome and safety valve cover, and it will be noticed that the locomotive is, by this date, equipped with vaccum brake hoses. No 726, a Northern Division locomotive, was withdrawn in July 1918.

83 GW no 13

No 13 was a 'one off' built at Swindon in October 1886 to lot 72, works number 1094. The driving wheels were 4ft 0in diameter and the cylinders 16 × 21in. The photograph was taken before December 1897 when no 13 was rebuilt as a 4-4-0 tank engine. It was Swindon practice at this time to allot low running numbers to experimental designs and obviously no 13 was not considered satisfactory in its original form. It was withdrawn in May 1926. The probable intention of this design was to produce a short wheelbase locomotive suitable for working branch lines and goods yards with sharp curves. The total wheelbase was only 18ft 0in, and the tanks were at the back and underneath. It was used on the Abingdon and St Ives branches.

82 GW Metro tank The Metro tank engines were of several different classes and variations, and were built over a long period of time between 1869 and 1899, all having the same purpose of working the Metropolitan lines in London where the GW had running powers. Many were fitted with condensers for working in the underground sections. No 1413 was Swindon lot no 47, works no 746, built in August 1878 and was of 1401 class, the first 'metros' to be designed by William Dean. Three different classes had already been built by Armstrong, all being in batches of twenty. Driving wheels of 1401 class were 5ft 1in diameter and the cylinders were 16 × 24in. No 1413 was withdrawn in March 1931.

85 GW 1076 class

No 1282 was one of a large class of 266 locomotives known as 1076 class, although when originally built they were in three classes, 1076, 727 and 1134.

No 1282 was built at Swindon to lot 45, works number 717 in December 1877, to 1134 class. The photograph shows the locomotive after pannier tanks had replaced the original saddle tanks in April 1916. At this time it was equipped with a spark-arresting chimney for working in the military stores department at Didcot, along with seven other locomotives. The spark arresters were removed later and the photograph almost certainly dates to April 1916 when the new tank was fitted. Driving wheels were nominally 4ft 6in diameter and cylinders 17 × 24in. No 1282 was withdrawn in December 1936.

84 GW 119 class

119 class, to which no 126 belonged, were renewals of earlier tender engines and were built at Wolverhampton to lots 4 and 5, no 126 being turned out in March 1881. The photograph shows the locomotive as it appeared before reboilering in December 1898. Subsequently its appearance was greatly changed when it was fitted with pannier tanks in October 1920, and it was withdrawn in July 1928. Cylinders were 17 × 24in and driving wheels a nominal 4ft 6in diameter. Each locomotive of the class exceeded a million miles of running before withdrawal.

86 GW 1076 class

The later pannier tank version of the 1076 class is again shown here but with standard chimney. No 1659 was the penultimate locomotive to be built (originally as 1134 class) at Swindon in May 1881 to Swindon lot 55, works number 864. It was rebuilt from saddle tank to pannier tank in May 1916. Note the bucket hanging on the rear bunker, which was a common sight on GW 0-6-0 tank locomotives generally. No 1659 was withdrawn from traffic in October 1930.

87 GW 2021 class

No 2048 was a Wolverhampton-built locomotive, to 2021 class, with smaller driving wheels of 4ft 1½in diameter and 16½ × 24in cylinders. 2021 was a numerous class of 140 engines built during 1897–1905. No 2048 was built at Wolverhampton to lot 63 in August 1898, and retained a saddle tank until February 1948 when, as BR 2048, it was fitted with a pannier tank and not withdrawn until May 1952.

88 GW 3001 class

As on other railways in the 1890s, there was a revival of locomotives with single driving wheels and a class of thirty 2-2-2s were built in 1891-2, known as 3001 class. Eight were built as broad gauge, with the wheels outside both sets of the double frames to be converted later to standard gauge. No 3004, however, was built to the standard gauge at Swindon to lot 84, works number 1224 in February 1892. Driving wheels were 7ft 8½in diameter and cylinders 20 × 24in. All carried names, no 3004 being *Black Prince*. They were found to be too heavy at the front end, and following a derailment of one of them they were rebuilt in 1894 as 4-2-2s, no 3004 being altered in October of that year. The photograph shows the locomotive in 2-2-2 form. As 4-2-2s they became part of 3031 *Achilles* class. No 3004 was withdrawn in October 1911.

This locomotive was originally numbered 3300 until 1912, and was of *Badminton* (originally 3292) class. Named *Hotspur*, it was built in July 1898 at Swindon under lot 109 to works number 1600. These locomotives were the first on the GWR to have Belpaire fireboxes. 18 × 26in cylinders and 6ft 8in diameter driving wheels were fitted. In October 1911 no 3300 was superheated and, renumbered 4108 in 1912, it was fitted with piston valves in April 1915. The boiler seen in this post-1912 photograph was the third one to be fitted on this locomotive, all three being of different types. It was withdrawn from service in March 1930.

89 GW 3031 *Achilles* **class**

This photograph shows the 3031 class to which the 3001 2-2-2s were rebuilt
being no 3031 *Achilles* itself. Driving wheels were of the same size as the 3001
class but the cylinders were one inch smaller in diameter, being 19 × 24in.
No 3031 was built at Swindon in March 1894 and was no 1391 of lot 94 in
the works. The engines received world-wide acclaim, but as with other singles
they had relatively short lives as train weights got too heavy for them. By the
end of 1915 none were left, no 3031 being withdrawn in July 1912.

91 GW 3700 *City* **class**

As its name *City of Bristol* suggests, these engines were known as *City* class or, after the 1912 renumbering, sometimes referred to as 3700 class. No 3435 is seen here with its original number before being changed to 3712. It was built in May 1903 as Swindon works number 1995 of lot 141, and had 6ft 8½in diameter driving wheels and 18 × 26in cylinders. All the *Cities* were later superheated, No 3435 in January 1912, and in 1915 as 3712 it was fitted with piston valves. The famous *City of Truro*, now preserved, was one of this class and as a whole they achieved a reputation for high speeds. No 3712 was withdrawn in May 1931.

94 GW *Saint* **class**

This was the prototype for a famous class, the *Saints*, built from 1902–13. This photograph is from the period between February 1902 when the locomotive was built, and June 1902. It was then named *Dean* before being changed to *William Dean* in November of that year, in honour of the recently retired locomotive engineer who was now succeeded by his assistant, G.J. Churchward. It was Swindon works number 1908 of lot 132, and it differed from the later engines in framing, cylinders and valve gear. In June 1903 it was reboiled with a coned boiler. It was renumbered 2900 in 1912 having been superheated in April 1910. In addition to *Saint* names, the class also incorporated the *Lady* series of 1906 with slightly larger cylinders ($18\frac{1}{4} \times$ 30in), and the *Courts* with $18\frac{1}{2} \times$ 30in cylinders as well as the *Albion* series of 1903 with the original $18 \times$ 30in cylinders. No 2900 was withdrawn in June 1932.

92 GW 3300 *Bulldog* **class**

The 3300 or *Bulldog* class was a large one with three main variations: those with curved frames, straight frames and straight deep frames. In addition to the frames there were variations in the boilers; some of them had domes and some were domeless at different periods, and both parallel and coned boilers were used. No 3390 carried the number 3452 until 1912 and was one of the first of the class to have the coned boiler. As will be seen it had a straight frame when built at Swindon in October 1903 to lot 142, works number 2012. It was superheated in December 1910 and in May 1927 the name *Wolverhampton* was removed because of confusion with train destinations. It was withdrawn in March 1939.

93 GW 3300 *Bulldog* **class**

This was also of the same class as *Wolverhampton,* and also straight-framed with coned domeless boiler, but it carries its pre-1912 number. After 1912 it became 3404. Its name was *Barbados* and it was Swindon no 2049, lot 148 of March 1904. It was superheated in August 1910 and was withdrawn in September 1937. The driving wheels of this class were 5ft 8in diameter and the cylinders 18 × 26in. They were originally employed on secondary express trains.

This was also of the *Saint* class, being of the *Albion* series of 1903–5. It carries its original number in this photograph; it was renumbered 2973 in 1912 and bore the name *Robins Bolitho* (a GWR director). It was turned out of Swindon in March 1903, and was works number 2107 of lot 154. In October 1910 it was fitted with a superheated boiler. These locomotives, and subsequent ones, always had the coned boiler of two types, long and short. The driving wheels on all of them were 6ft 8½in diameter. No 2973 was withdrawn in July 1933.

96 GW *Saint* **class**
As will be inferred from its name *Lady of the Lake*, no 2902 was of the *Lady* series. Cylinders of this series were originally 18¼in diameter but the 18½in size later became the standard for all the engines of this class. No 2902 was built at Swindon in May 1906, and its works number was 2200 of lot 164. It was not named, however, until April 1907. In February 1910 it received its superheated boiler and it was one of forty-seven out of the total of seventy-seven built that survived into British Railways stock as BR 2902, being withdrawn in August 1949. GW engines retained their original numbers on BR.

97 GW 3600 class

Although not the only class of GW 2-4-2 tank engine, this was the only class built in any large numbers and was known as 3600 class. There were thirty-one of them built at Swindon from 1900 to 1903. Those built up to 1902 originally had parallel boilers, but the 1903 ones to lot 143 (of which 3626 was works number 2018 of December 1903) were built with coned boilers which then became standard for the whole of the class. Driving wheels were 5ft 2in diameter and cylinders 17 × 24in. All were later superheated, no 3626 in March 1922, and this locomotive was withdrawn in August 1932.

98 GW *County* tanks

These were known as *County* tanks or 2221 class and were used on the more important suburban trains. They were a tank engine version of the *County* class 4-4-0s, with the same cylinder dimensions of 18 × 30in and wheels of 6ft 8½in diameter the largest then in use on tank engines. No 2234 was Swindon-built in October 1908 to lot 175, works number 2323. It was superheated in July 1910. For the most part, the class worked in the London area hauling fast services to Reading as well as other services to High Wycombe, Oxford, Hungerford and Aylesbury. This particular locomotive was withdrawn in January 1932.

99 GW 3100 class

Originally known as 3100 class built in 1903–6, this class consisted of forty engines but they were greatly increased in numbers from 1929 to 1949, when no less than 140 more were built. 5ft 8in diameter wheels were used with 18 × 30in cylinders. No 3121 was built at Swindon in May 1905 to lot 152, works number 2086. It had a superheated boiler from December 1911. From 1928, in anticipation of the building of new locomotives, the original ones were all renumbered in the 5100 series and the number of this locomotive was changed to 5121 in May 1929. It became BR 5121 in 1948, but was withdrawn in October of that year.

100 GW 3100 class

Also of 3100 class, no 3141 was built in March 1906 at Swindon and was part of lot 159, works number 2148. It was fitted with a superheated boiler in December 1910 and was renumbered 5141 in January 1929. It had a longer life than 3121, surviving as BR 5141 until October 1952. Of the original forty engines, twenty-nine passed into BR stock and the last of these was withdrawn in 1955. As might be expected, the locomotives built later lasted longer, but all had gone by the end of 1961.

9
Welsh Railways
and others connected
with the Great Western

The South Wales Railways were all principally concerned with coal traffic down the valleys and much of this went to other railways, as the Welsh coalfields produced what was known as good 'steam coal'. In the steam age coal passed down the valley lines every few minutes throughout the day.

The largest of these railways was the Taff Vale Railway with $124\frac{1}{2}$ route miles, but with an operating stock of more than twice that number of locomotives. It was also the oldest, having been established in 1836, and in the late nineteenth century its dividends reached $17\frac{1}{2}$ per cent.

From 1863 until his death in 1911, its locomotive engineer was Tom Hurry Riches. At the time of his appointment he was the youngest locomotive engineer in Britain, being then not quite twenty-seven years old. His principal locomotives were the 0–6–0s of K and L classes. The K class was also adopted by Barton Wright as a standard for the Lancashire and Yorkshire railway. However, some of these were rebuilt as saddle tank locomotives to E class (plate 101). The original design was Sharp Stewart's standard one as supplied to the Furness Railway (plate 56) and the Cambrian Railway.

The 0–6–2 tank was also introduced into Wales following Barton Wright's adoption of this arrangement for the L & Y (plate 41), and the N class of 1891 were ten in number (plate 102). The class G 0–6–0 tank engines, originally designed for the Metropolitan Railway in London, were a chance purchase but were very suitable for the Taff Vale traffic (plate 103).

The Cardiff Railway was principally a dock railway with thirty-two locomotives in operation from 1908. All were tank engines (plate 104).

Another dock railway was the Alexandra (Newport and South Wales) Docks and Railway with thirty-five locomotives in use from 1908 and these, also were all tank engines (plates 105-7).

The Rhondda and Swansea Bay Railway was promoted to export coal through Port Talbot and Briton Ferry, and opened in 1885. There were $28\frac{3}{4}$ route miles and, after 1904, thirty-seven locomotives. However, additional locomotives came to the line from the Great Western after 1907 (plate 108). The Kitson 0–6–2 tank engines were the newest locomotives on the line (plate 109) dating from 1899, although there had been an earlier one of this class purchased in 1885. Again, only tank engines were employed.

The Barry Dock and Railway Company, more often just known as the Barry Railway, had 68 route miles and was incorporated in 1884 by dissatisfied traders who claimed that Cardiff docks and the Taff Vale railway were not developing fast enough to cope with the growing coal traffic. By 1905 it was operating 138 locomotives.

The E class six-coupled tank engines (plate 110) were to Hudswell Clarke's standard design. This firm was founded in 1860 by W.S. Hudswell and John Clarke who had been works manager at Kitson's for some years. Becoming Hudswell Clarke and Company in 1880, it built many tank engines until 1961, supplying the Rhymney, Cardiff, Port Talbot, and Taff railways, the Port of London Authority, Manchester Ship Canal Company and many others.

The J class 2-4-2 tank engines (plate 112), however, incorporated several standard components from the G class 0-4-4 tank engines of 1892-5 designed by the company's engineer, J.H. Hosgood. The F class (plate 111) was essentially a saddle tank version of the A class 0-6-0 tank engine built in 1888.

There were forty-two engines of B1 class (plate 114) built by Sharp Stewart, Vulcan Foundry, and the last five as illustrated by SA Franco Belge of La Croyère in Belgium, the last of these being exhibited at the Paris exhibition in 1900. The 0-8-0s of class D, another chance purchase, (plate 113) were the only tender engines on the line.

The Rhymney Railway played an important part in the South Wales railway system. Although it had only fifty-one miles of track it had a total of one hundred locomotives by 1910 and 127 before its amalgamation with the GW in 1923.

From 1861 the railway, first opened in 1858, had the services of a remarkable man, Cornelius Lundie, who combined the positions of general manager, superintendent and engineer, continuing to direct the operation of the railway until 1905 when he was eighty-seven years old.

After the introduction of the 0-6-2 saddle tank engines (plates 115, 116) originally known as 57 class, a side tank 0-6-2 design on more modern lines was brought out in 1904 (plate 117). Construction of these and an 0-6-0 tank engine design of 1908 were continued by C.T. Hurry Riches, the son of Tom Hurry Riches of the Taff Vale Railway, who succeeded Cornelius Lundie. He also designed the rail motor tank engines (plate 118). His father was a keen proponent of steam motors, and had built several for the Taff Vale Railway. Many other railways at this time did the same to combat competition from electric tramcars.

The Port Talbot Railway and Docks had a route mileage of $33\frac{1}{2}$ miles. It was opened in 1897-8 and its locomotives were mostly built between 1896 and 1901, although three earlier second-hand locomotives were disposed of in 1897 and 1910 and two four-coupled tank engines, purchased from the Barry Railway, were built in 1890.

The arrival of the 0-8-2 tank engines from Sharp Stewart and Co (plate 119) made four 0-6-2 tank engines redundant, and these were sold in 1902-03. The locomotive stock was then twenty-two; eight 0-6-0 tank engines, five 0-8-2 tank engines, two four-coupled tank engines (ex-Barry Railway) and seven 0-6-2 tank engines. In addition there was a rail motor which was sold to the Port of London Authority in 1921.

The Cambrian Railway was much larger, having 295¼ route miles, but, serving rural areas in mid-Wales, had nothing like the same density of traffic and its operating stock of locomotives never exceeded 100.

It connected in the North with the Great Western at Wrexham and the L & NW at Whitchurch to Oswestry, where the locomotive works were situated, and then to Welshpool where it joined the GW/L & NW joint line from Shrewsbury.

From Llanidloes an absorbed railway, the Mid Wales, ran to Brecon connecting with the Brecon and Merthyr Railway. The main line ran on to Machynlleth and Aberystwyth, with the coast line branching off at Dovey Junction to Barmouth and Pwllheli, making a connection at Afon Wen with the L & NW branch from Menai Bridge. The line from Shrewsbury to Aberystwyth and Pwllheli is still open.

The locomotive engineer from 1884 was William Aston who was an apprentice at Sharp Stewart, and worked under Ramsbottom at Crewe. He adopted the Cambrian Locomotive livery of 'invisible green', a greenish black. The 61 class (plate 120) was his second class of 4-4-0 locomotives and by 1904 there were twenty-four of them. The design of the bogie side-tank class (plate 121) was Nasmyth Wilson's. The branch to Wrexham for which they were intended was opened at the same time.

James Nasmyth, who built the first steam hammer in 1839 at his Patricroft works near Manchester, retired in 1857 and Robert Wilson entered the business. Locomotives had been built in small numbers since 1839 and 1,307 were turned out between 1873 and 1938, 1,118 of them for export.

The Lambourn Valley Railway locomotives (plates 122, 123) were purchased from the Great Western Railway by Herbert Jones who succeeded Aston as the Cambrian Railway's locomotive engineer in 1899. He had been on the Midland Railway, and naturally introduced many Midland practices to the Cambrian.

As the Lambourn Valley Railway had such a short independent existence the locomotives were in good condition, *Eadweade* being practically new. The Cambrian Railway removed the names and gave them the numbers of withdrawn locomotives.

Chapman and Furneaux of Gateshead who built the first two had been Black, Hawthorn and Company until 1896, who had taken over from R. Coulthard and Company in 1865. This original firm started building locomotives in 1835. The Hunslet Engine Company in Leeds, the builders of the third locomotive, was founded in 1864. Of all the steam locomotive builders, this firm is the only one successfully to survive the change to internal combustion technology, and is still in business today.

The Midland and South Western Junction Railway had twenty-eight locomotives in use by 1910. In all there were ten 4-4-0s, an earlier one having been supplied in 1893 in addition to the North British Locomotive Company ones (plate 124). There were also ten 0-6-0s. In addition, 2-6-0s and 2-4-0s were also employed, and a number of tank engines of various types including two handsome side tank engines of 4-4-4 arrangement.

The Alexandra Docks, Barry, Cambrian, Cardiff, Rhymney and Taff Vale railways were amalgamated with the Great Western Railway on 1 January 1923. The other companies were absorbed by the Great Western as subsidiaries in 1922, except for the M & SWJ which was absorbed on 1 July 1923.

103 Taff Vale (ex-Metropolitan) G class

Together with four others like it, this powerful outside-framed tank engine was built originally for the Metropolitan Railway in London by the Worcester Engine Co in 1868 (works number 38). They were for working a proposed steeply-graded extension from St Johns Wood to Hampstead, but this was not built and the five locomotives were put up for sale in 1873. Two were purchased by the Taff Vale in that year and a further two in 1874, the fifth locomotive being sold to the Sirhowy Railway in 1873. No 99 was purchased in November 1874, and was Metropolitan no 37. On the TVR it became no 99 in 1875. It had 4ft 0in diameter driving wheels, 20 × 24in cylinders and when purchased had no cab and was fitted with condensing equipment. It was rebuilt in 1881 as seen here, with $17\frac{1}{2}$ × 24in cylinders; from about 1892 it was regarded as G class and was withdrawn in 1898.

101 Taff Vale E class

This locomotive was one of four built by Sharp Stewart and Co in 1873; they were to Sharp's standard design as supplied to the Furness and the Cambrian Railways being later classified as E on the Taff Vale. In 1891–2 they were rebuilt as saddle tank engines and were transferred to 'surplus stock' (the TVR's terms for duplicate list). No 264 was originally no 87 (Sharp Stewart number 2282) and was renumbered 264 in April 1891. In 1922 the number 795 was allotted to it on the GWR, but it was decided to withdraw it in July 1923 and the number plate was probably not put on.

102 Taff Vale N class

Of more recent date, this was one of ten locomotives built in 1891 by Kitson and Co (works number 3384) with 4ft 6in diameter driving wheels and 17½ × 26in cylinders. On the TVR they were classified as N. It was reboilered in March 1919. It passed to the GW in 1923, becoming GW 495, and was withdrawn in September 1928. It was similar to the earlier M and M1 classes of Taff Vale 0-6-2T. They worked some passenger trains, but were employed principally on the coal traffic which of course was very heavy on the TVR. This railway was the largest and longest-established of the South Wales railways grouped with the GW in 1922.

104 Cardiff Railway

This locomotive was the personal property of the Marquis of Bute's Trustees when it was built by a general engineering firm near the Bute West Dock, opened in Cardiff by the second Marquis in 1839 as an outlet for coal. Locomotives to shunt in the dock sidings were for some years provided by the Taff Vale Railway, but from 1860 the marquis provided his own locomotives. The builders were Parfitt and Jenkins, and they built thirteen locomotives for the marquis, but not for any other railway. Dates of building are uncertain, but no 12 was probably built in 1871–2. The dock became the Bute Docks Co in 1886, changing its name to the Cardiff Railway in 1897. No 12 became GW 694 in 1922, and was put on the 'sales list' in October 1926.

105 Alexandra Docks and Railway

The Alexandra (Newport and South Wales) Docks and Railway owned the Alexandra docks in Newport (then in Monmouthshire, now in Gwent). No 13 was one of mitivetwo built in 1884 by R & W Hawthorn and Co (works number 1976) with 18 × 24in cylinders and 4ft 0in diameter driving wheels. It became GW 665 in 1922, and was withdrawn in September 1926. The company owned $9\frac{1}{4}$ miles of railway between Newport and Pontypridd connected by running powers over the Brecon and Merthyr Railway in addition to 100 miles or so of dock sidings in Newport.

106 AD & R Peckett tank

Peckett and Sons (formerly Fox Walker and Co) of Bristol built this compact 0–6–0 saddle tank engine in 1890 and, with another supplied in the following year, they were of Peckett's standard industrial design. As will be seen, the AD & R company managed to get the full, rather lengthy title on to their number plates. This one was Peckett's number 465, and was no 18 on the AD & R, the other Peckett being no 19. They became GW nos 679 and 680 in 1922. No 679 was used at Weymouth for a few months by the GW before being sold in November 1929. It was resold several times, surviving until September 1953 at Trimsaran Colliery. The other one was withdrawn in December 1948.

107 AD & R Stephenson saddle tank

Possibly taken in 1898 when it was new, this photograph is interesting in that it shows a livery variation with the number painted on the tank side, surmounted by a crown instead of the usual number plate, but this may have been a temporary change. No 2 was one of five built in 1898 and 1900 by R. Stephenson and Co, replacing earlier locomotives purchased, second-hand, from the L & NW. It was Stephenson works no 2894 of May 1898. The wheels were 4ft 0½in diameter and the cylinders 16 × 24in. In 1922 it became GW 675 and was withdrawn in June 1926.

RHONDDA AND SWANSEA BAY (ex GW)

108

This railway ran from Treherbert to Port Talbot, Neath and Swansea. The GW obtained a controlling interest in the Railway in 1906, but it was not completely absorbed until 1 January 1922. The GW transferred seven locomotives to the R & SB in 1907, followed by three more in 1908, and there were further transfers in 1912, 1914, 1920 and 1921. No 33, a standard saddle tank engine built at Swindon in 1874 (works number 533, lot 37) was transferred in March 1914 reassuming its original number, 957, when returned to GW stock in December 1921. It was withdrawn in 1932.

109 Rhondda and Swansea Bay

The R & SB owned nineteen 0-6-2 tank engines, seventeen built by Kitson and Co between 1885 and 1904. No 20 was built in October 1899 and was Kitson works number 3883. It was one of twelve with 18 × 26in cylinders and 4ft 6in diameter coupled wheels with 3ft 8¼in diameter radial trailing wheels. After assuming control of the company in 1906, the GW reboilered these locomotives with Swindon boilers, that of no 20 being fitted in May 1908. It became GW 177 in 1922, and was withdrawn in June 1935.

BARRY RAILWAY

110 Barry E class

The Barry Railway served Bridgend, Pontypridd and Cardiff with services centred on Barry and, with the Taff Vale and the Rhymney was one of the three largest South Wales railways. No 51 was of E class, which was five 0-6-0 tank engines built by Hudswell Clarke of Leeds and designed for dock work with the ability to negotiate sharp curves. The wheels were 3ft 3½in and the cylinders 14 × 20in. It was built as works number 344 in January 1890. It was the last survivor of the class, becoming GW 784 in 1922 and BR 784 in 1948, being withdrawn in August 1949. By this time this small tank engine had travelled over 866,000 miles.

111 Barry F class

Class F, illustrated in this photograph, was a larger class of twenty-eight locomotives built by Sharp Stewart, Vulcan Foundry and North British Locomotive Co from 1890–1905. They were employed on heavy shunting work at Barry docks. No 47 was built by Sharp Stewart and Co in January 1890 and was the first of the class. It was renumbered 710 by the GW in 1922. They were not originally fitted with vacuum brakes, although some had become so by 1922. The GW rebuilt 710 in April 1924 and again in March 1930, and it was withdrawn in May 1932.

113 Barry D class

These eight-coupled engines were interesting in that they were the first such to be used on a British railway in regular traffic, and the only tender engines on the Barry Railway. They were built, with eighteen others, for the Swedish and Norwegian Railway in 1887–8 to Sharp Stewart's own design but were returned to the makers as the S & N could not pay for them. Sixteen were sold to two railways in Germany, and the other four (two of which had been held back in this country pending payment) were sold to the Barry Railway after prolonged litigation in 1889 and 1897, where they became D class. No 93 was Sharp Stewart number 3394 purchased in March 1897. Wheels were 4ft 3in diameter and the cylinders 20 × 26in. It was given the GW no 1390, and withdrawn in April 1930.

112 Barry J class

There were eleven 2-4-2 tank engines of class J on the Barry Railway, and they were built by Hudswell Clarke and Sharp Stewart and Co between 1897 and 1899. No 88 was one of the first three built by Hudswell Clarke, makers number 475, in May 1897. Coupled wheels were 5ft 7½in diameter and the cylinders 18 × 26in. There were differences between the locomotives of the two manufacturers, consisting of the pitch of the boiler and the shape of the cab, and for a while the Sharp locomotives were known as class J1. No 88 became GW 1313, and was withdrawn in May 1928. They were used on the busy Cardiff suburban service and, as can be seen, had polished brass domes.

114 Barry B1 class

No 124 was of the B1 class, the largest class on the Barry Railway. It was built in Belgium by SA Franco Belge (their number 1274) in April 1900. The locomotives of B class, also of the same wheel arrangement, were rebuilt with similar boilers to the B1s by 1903, and they were then all regarded simply as B class. They were mixed traffic engines working both passenger and mineral trains. The cylinders, 18 × 26in when built, were latterly 17½in diameter. As Gw 275, the former 124 was rebuilt at Swindon in July 1924 and was not withdrawn until April 1948.

RHYMNEY RAILWAY

115 Rhymney K class
The Rhymney Railway ran from Cardiff through Caerphilly to Merthyr, Dowlais and Rhymney and made contact with other Welsh railways, the LNWR and GW. These outside frame 0-6-2 tank engines were enlarged versions of earlier 0-6-0 tank engines, and were built in seven batches by four manufacturers, there being forty-seven of them in all built from 1890-1900. No 74 was a Sharp Stewart product of 1894 (their number 4042). The cylinders were $17\frac{1}{2} \times 24$in and the coupled wheels were 4ft 7in diameter. In 1906 they were classified as K class and the number was transferred to the cab side on a small plate. Becoming GW 107 in 1922, it was put on the 'sales list' in November 1927, only to be scrapped in December 1928.

116 Rhymney K class
This locomotive was of the same class as no 74, but photographed after 1909. It shows the number painted on the tank side with the letters 'RR' on either side of it, which was the method adopted instead of plates. No 94 was built by Hudswell Clarke (works number 548) in 1900. On the GW its number was 137 and it was put on the 'sales list' and scrapped on the same dates as the former no 74. The Rhymney used the Westinghouse brake on its own stock but also had some vacuum-fitted locomotives for use on other companies' stock. Both this locomotive and no 74 were Westinghouse fitted. The engines were painted dark Brunswick green with chocolate coloured frames.

117 Rhymney M class

Of more modern design, no 106 was the first of six 0-6-2 tank engines built by R. Stephenson and Co in 1904, being delivered in June. When C.T. Hurry Riches took charge of the locomotives in January 1906, he introduced a classification scheme by letter and these became class M. Considerable difficulties with the boilers of these engines were encountered until they were fitted with R class boilers in 1917-20. As GW 47, this locomotive was fitted with a GW 5600 class boiler in July 1930, but no others of the class were so treated. It was withdrawn in April 1949 by British Railways and cut up the following September.

118 Rhymney Rail Motor Tank Engine

This locomotive and another, no 120, were originally built as 0-4-0 tank engines with an extension of the frame at the rear to support one end of rail motor carriages. They were built by Hudswell Clarke with Walschearts valve gear, and were delivered in September 1907. The carriage part was built by Cravens Ltd of Sheffield and the two units were numbered 1 and 2. As with most of these combined engine and carriages introduced about this time, trouble was experienced with vibration and rough riding, and they were converted into 0-6-0 back tanks or 'trailing tanks', as the RR referred to it, as seen here. It was renumbered 121 in June 1919, withdrawn in June 1925 as GW 662, and cut up three months later.

CAMBRIAN RAILWAY

120 Cambrian 61 class

The Cambrian Railway comprised about 300 miles of rural lines in mid-Wales. Passenger traffic in the summer could be quite heavy. These 4-4-0 locomotives were built by Sharp Stewart and Co in 1893-5, and were known as 'Large Bogie Passenger Class'. This locomotive was Sharp Stewart number 3901, and was the first of the class numbered 61 on the Cambrian. Driving wheels were 6ft 0in diameter and in 1922, when the GW took over, it was renumbered as here 1088. It will be noticed that although the GW plate has been affixed the tender is still lettered 'Cambrian'. It was withdrawn in March 1926. Further locomotives of this class were built by R. Stephenson and Co in 1897-8, and two by the Cambrian Railway works in 1901 and 1904.

119 Port Talbot Railway and Docks

There were three of these large locomotives at Port Talbot built by Sharp Stewart late in 1901 and put into Port Talbot Railway stock as numbers 17-19 in 1902. They were similar to ones supplied to the Barry Railway in 1896. The boilers were 13ft 3in long and the wheelbase 22ft 11in in all. No 18 became GW 1359 in 1922; the bunkers were altered to GW standard pattern and new smokeboxes in place of the old ones (which had given trouble hitherto) were fitted. This locomotive was withdrawn in December 1935, but the former no 17, as GW 1358, was not withdrawn until 1948.

121 Cambrian 8 class

This 'Bogie Side Tank' class was built for working the Wrexham and Ellesmere branch in 1895 and 1899 by Nasmyth Wilson and Co. No 9 was no 559 in the makers' works, and this class consisted of six engines, three built in 1895 and nos 8, 9 and 23 in 1899, no 9 being delivered in June. The coupled wheels were 5ft 3in diameter and 17 × 24in cylinders were fitted. The numbers were of raised brass. Three of the class were withdrawn in 1922, but no 9 survived until June 1928 as GW 20.

122 Cambrian (ex-Lambourne Valley)

This photograph shows the third locmotive built for the Lambourne Valley Railway in 1903 by the Hunslet Engine Co (works number 811) and originally named *Eadweade*. The GW absorbed this railway in 1905, and its three locomotives were sold by them to the Cambrian. This locomotive is seen here as Cambrian no 24 about 1922–3 but it has already been lettered GWR before the fitting of its GW number plate, when it became 819. It had 13 × 18in cylinders and 3ft 7in diameter wheels. It survived much longer than the two earlier Lambourne Valley locomotives (one of which is shown in the next illustration), and was not withdrawn until March 1946.

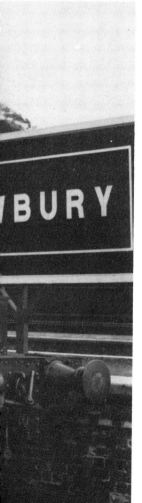

123 Lambourne Valley

This twelve-mile railway, opened in 1898, connected with the GW at Newbury and this photograph of *Eahlswith* standing at Newbury was taken sometime during 1898–1905 before the take-over by the GW. With the locomotive in the previous photograph, and another named *Aelfred*, all three were sold to the Cambrian who removed the names. *Eahlswith* had 12 × 20in cylinders, and all three were 0-6-0 tank engines with 3ft 7in diameter wheels. On the Cambrian Railway it became no 26, becoming GW property again in 1922 with the number 820. It was withdrawn in March 1930 and sold in March 1931. The builders were Chapman and Furneaux of Gateshead (formerly Black Hawthorn and Co) and the works number was 1161.

124 Midland and South Western Junction

The M & SW Jct was originally the Swindon, Marlborough and Andover Railway but extended north to the Banbury-Cheltenham line at Andoversford and the line was a valuable link for north-south traffic. This 4-4-0 class consisted of nine locomotives built by the North British Locomotive Co between 1905 and 1914 with 5ft 9in diameter coupled wheels and 18 × 26in cylinders. Seen here as GW 1120 after rebuilding in February 1928 with a standard GW boiler, it was M & SW Jct no 2 and North British Locomotive Co number 18791 built in 1909.

10
Railways of the South of England

London and South Western Railway

First opened in 1838 as the London and Southampton Railway and reaching Southampton in 1840, by which time the name had been changed, the L & SW extended to Portsmouth in 1848, Salisbury in 1857, Exeter in 1860 and Bournemouth in 1870. It took over the Southampton and Dorchester Railway in 1848, enabling it to reach Weymouth, and the North Devon Railway in 1862. It extended the latter beyond Barnstaple to Ilfracombe and Torrington, and had branches to Bude and Padstow, opening its own line to Plymouth in 1876. It was thus very much in competition with the Great Western Railway. Its London terminus at Waterloo was opened in 1848 and it had a network of suburban lines in south London and Surrey.

Joseph Beattie became the locomotive engineer in 1850. He was an inventive engineer and held many patents including a feed-water heating apparatus and a coal-burning firebox. He extended the locomotive works, then at Nine Elms in London, and he was influenced by his predecessor J.V. Gooch who favoured fairly light locomotives with outside cylinders. Six-coupled goods engines, however, had inside cylinders (plate 125). These locomotives originally carried names and were known as *Lion* class, number 3 being named *Transit*.

The W.G. Beattie 302 class (plate 126) were the first from Beyer Peacock with inside frames, although as will be seen, the *Lion* class built at Nine Elms already had them.

William Adams came from the North London Railway (qv) and the Great Eastern. He had designed the first 2-6-0 *Mogul* type in Britain for the GE but these were not very successful. His designs for the L & SW, however, were very successful. His locomotives had large bearing surfaces and were simple and robust but with a graceful line, giving them long life, as will be noted from the 395 class main line goods (plates 128, 129). Following the success of 0-4-2 engines on the London, Brighton and South Coast Railway (plate 137) Adams designed two classes of 0-4-2 for the L & SW, the first of which came out in 1887, becoming known as *Jubilees* after the Royal Jubilee of that year.

Three of Adams' locomotives are preserved, a 4-4-0 at the National Railway Museum, York, a 4-4-2 tank engine on the Bluebell Railway and an 0-4-4 tank engine on the Isle of Wight.

London, Brighton and South Coast Railway

Opened in 1841 as the London and Brighton Railway, the name was changed in 1846 by amalgamation with the London and Croydon railway.

The system covered Sussex and the south coast between Havant and Hastings, and there was joint working with the South Eastern Railway between Croydon and Redhill. The London termini were at Victoria and London Bridge.

John Chester Craven, the locomotive engineer from 1847, had been apprenticed with Robert Stephenson and Company and his ability was such that he became a works manager for Shepherd and Todd in Leeds when still only twenty-six years old. Three years later, on the Manchester and Leeds Railway, he became a locomotive foreman. In 1845 he was appointed locomotive engineer to the Eastern Counties Railway (later the Great Eastern) before moving to the LBSC works at Brighton which he greatly enlarged. He positively opposed standardisation, believing that locomotives should be suited to their particular duties. Consequently there were numerous variations in his locomotives. He built seventy singles of twenty-one different types (plates 132-5). There were nine varieties of 0-6-0 goods engines of which the 249 class were the last (plate 136). When the board asked him to reduce the number of types, Craven, a stubborn and irascible man, flatly refused and resigned, William Stroudley being appointed in his place.

Stroudley advocated the Westinghouse brake which the LBSC adopted and he believed in large boilers. He introduced a standardisation policy, sweeping away Craven's numerous types, and started the naming of engines. One of the *Gladstone* class 0-4-2s (plate 137), number 189 *Edward Blount*, was shown at the Paris Exhibition in 1889. Stroudley unfortunately contracted influenza, which proved fatal, while conducting trials of this engine between Paris and Laroche. He was succeeded by R.J. Billinton.

Originally known as the East Kent Railway the London, Chatham & Dover Railway (plate 138) was opened between 1859 and 1861 giving a shorter route between Strood and Dover than that of the South Eastern Railway. It was soon extended to Victoria Station in London. After many years of bitter competition with the South Eastern Railway a joint committee of both companies was formed from 1st January 1899 and became known as the South Eastern & Chatham Railway.

126 LSW 302 class

The elder Beattie was succeeded by his son, W.G. Beattie, at Nine Elms. He did not however have the same ability as his father for designing locomotives, and relied on private manufacturers, particularly Beyer Peacock and Co (his father had been a personal friend of Charles Beyer) to produce new designs. This class of heavy goods engines, the 302 class, was built between 1874 and 1878. Hitherto outside frames had been used on goods engines, but these had inside frames. The wheels were 5ft 0in diameter and cylinders 17 × 24in. The original no 305 (Beyer Peacock No 1363) was renumbered 0305 in 1901, and was withdrawn in 1915. Seen here after rebuilding in August 1886, it was originally built in June 1874.

125 LSW Beattie Goods

In 1850 Joseph Hamilton Beattie replaced Joseph Gooch as the LSW Locomotive Superintendent at the original works of the company, at Nine Elms in London, and he remained in charge until his death in 1871. No 03 was one of a type of goods engine with 5ft 0in diameter wheels and $16\frac{1}{2} \times 22$in cylinders, first produced in 1863. Thirty-two were built up to 1873, this one being Nine Elms works no 75 of July 1870. Numbered originally 3, it became 03 when it was transferred to the duplicate list in 1894, and was sold in April 1897.

127 LSW 2-4-0 83 class

Of several classes of 2-4-0s constructed by Joseph Beattie No 86 *Shark* was one of twenty 83 class built between 1866 and 1871. They had 6ft 6in diameter driving wheels and 17 × 22in cylinders and ran for many years on the Waterloo to Portsmouth line. *Shark* was Nine ELms works No 42 of December 1867. It is seen here fitted with an Adams chimney so the photograph was taken between 1880 and 1894. It was placed on the duplicate list as 086 1891 and withdrawn in 1894.

128 LSW 395 class

The new Locomotive Superintendent following W.G. Beattie's resignation in 1877 was William Adams, and this large class of goods engines known as the 395 class was first introduced under him in 1881. In all, seventy were built between then and 1885. No 27 was built in November 1885 by Neilson and Co (works no 3453) and was put on the duplicate list in 1904. In 1916 it was sold to the War Department and sent to Palestine; later it was sold to the Palestine Railway. Note the lettering 'SWR' omitting the 'L'. It was scrapped in 1929.

William Adams's 135 class of 1880 consisted of twelve locomotives built by Beyer, Peacock & Co. They had 6ft 7in diameter driving wheels and 18 × 24in cylinders. No 141 was works No 1954. Notice the brass beading round the rim of the splashers with Beyer, Peacock's name, which was such a distinctive feature of the locomotives they built, rather like a Rolls-Royce radiator is today. This engine was replaced by Drummond 4-4-0s in 1902, although three others of the class survived until 1924.

129 LSW 395 class

Many of the 395 class became Southern Railway stock in 1923, and ex-LSW 101 is seen in this photograph as SR 3101 after 1933. The 395 class had 5ft 1in diameter coupled wheels and $17\frac{1}{2} \times 26$in cylinders. Comparing this photograph with that of no 27, which shows the class as they were first built, it will be seen that the Adams chimney and smokebox have been replaced by the Drummond type. Some locomotives of the class also had Drummond boilers fitted, and some had ex-South Eastern and Chatham boilers. The original boilers were also kept in use and periodically overhauled, as was the case with no 101. Under British Railways the number became 30566 and it was withdrawn in February 1959. The building date was December 1885 (Neilson number 3459).

Beyer, Peacock & Co supplied six of these 4-4-0Ts in 1875. As will be seen they were very similar to the 4-4-0Ts which they had already built for the Metropolitan and Metropolitan District Railways even though No 323 (works No 1359) is not seen here in original condition but as rebuilt in Adams's time. Apart from the change of chimney and removal of the Beattie feedwater heating and condensing apparatus (also fitted to some other classes) it has not changed much in appearance. They had 5ft 9in diameter driving wheels and 17 × 24in cylinders and were used in London on Metropolitan and suburban services and in the Plymouth area. No 323, the last of the class to be completed was placed on the duplicate list in 1900 and withdrawn in 1906.

LONDON, BRIGHTON AND SOUTH COAST RAILWAY

132 LBSC Craven Single
Built at Brighton works by the LBSC company, this and no 196 replaced two locomotives sold to the Egyptian State Railway. They were both built in November 1865. Brighton works were at this time under the superintendency of John Chester Craven, who had been in charge since 1847. The locomotive is seen in original condition, but the name *Glynde* was not applied until after Craven's retirement in 1869 when he was succeeded by William Stroudley. No 194 later became no 484 (in 1888) and was scrapped in 1892.

134 LBSC Craven single

Four singles were built in October and November 1866 at Brighton, with 6ft
0in diameter wheels and 16 × 20in cylinders, for the Portsmouth service. No
233 was built in October and was Brighton works no 136. It was named
Horsham by Stroudley and renumbered 487 in 1882. The following year it was
sold, with no 474 *Dorking*, to the West Lancashire Railway, subsequently
absorbed by the Lancashire and Yorkshire Railway. The photograph was
taken on the WLR where no 487 became no 6 and no 474 became 5. Note
that the WLR retained the name, and the new number plates were supplied
by Brighton works.

133 LBSC Craven Single

No 196 was built at Brighton at the same time as no 194, in November 1865
and the dimensions of both were the same: 6ft 6in diameter driving wheels
and 17 × 22in cylinders. Craven, a stern disciplinarian, much feared by
employees, tended to build locomotives in ones and twos. Indeed, he is
credited with ordering some sixty-seven different types, only a couple of
which ever numbered more than ten. No 196 is seen here at the same period
as no 194, after being named *Pevensey* by Stroudley but before being
numbered 485 in 1888. It was scrapped in 1890.

135 LBSC 236 class

236 class consisted of six engines supplied by Nasmyth, Wilson and Co in 1867, with 6ft 6in diameter driving wheels. No 236 was built in April 1867 to Nasmyth works no 114. This one and the two others had slightly smaller cylinders than the three others supplied by Nasmyth's in June. No 236 was named *Arundel* by Stroudley and renumbered 476 in 1881 as seen here. The safety valve of the Salter type was situated on the brass dome and can be seen 'blowing off' here. The locomotive was broken up in December 1889. The engine sheds of the 'roundhouse' type are clearly seen in this photograph (see also plate 137) and the flower bed in front of the turntable is a nice touch.

136 LBSC 249 class

This was one of Craven's 249 class of which six were built by the Avonside Engine Co. No 472, originally no 253 until 1881, was the fifth of these, being numbered 748 in the Avonside works in Bristol and built in October 1868. They had 5ft 0in diameter wheels and 17 × 24in cylinders, and differed from previous designs in having deep slotted frames instead of open frames with tie bars. Notice the crude cab, little more than a weatherboard bent round at the corners. No 472 was scrapped in April 1896.

138 London, Chatham & Dover Railway 2-4-0T No 145

No 145 was originally built in 1856 by Sharp Stewart & Cø as a 2-4-0 with 5ft 6in diameter wheels and 15 × 20in cylinders for the Dutch Rhenish Railway. Along with five others it was purchased by the LC & DR in 1861 and until 1875 bore only the name *Onyx* as LC & DR engines were not numbered until then. In 1875 it was numbered 65 and renumbered 145 in 1876. In 1877 it was rebuilt as a 2-4-0T as seen here and in 1891 it was withdrawn.

137 LBSC B1 class

William Stroudley, who was only 37 when he came to the LBSC in 1870 from the Highland Railway, made his name there and his locomotive designs were quite unique at the time. Several famous classes were built under his supervision. This class, the B1 or *Gladstone* class, was one of the most famous. *Gladstone* itself is now preserved. They were built from 1882–91. No 174 was built at Brighton works in December 1890, and named *Fratton*. Without leading bogies the driving wheels had all but 10 tons of the total weight of 38.7 tons available for adhesion, giving them excellent haulage power. Put on the duplicate list as B174 by the Southern in 1923, the locomotive was withdrawn in April 1929 and scrapped in 1930.

Index